MAKE TIME

STRATEGIES FOR TIME EFFICIENCY AND FULFILLMENT

JAVIER ORTIZ

ST. JAMES PRESS

To Jessica, my guiding star and unwavering support, and to Isabella, our bright and beautiful daughter — you both illuminate my world and inspire every word I write. Thank you for the endless love and precious moments we share. This book is a tribute to the time we cherish together.

Lost time is never found again.

— BENJAMIN FRANKLIN

CONTENTS

Preface   xi
Introduction   xix

1. OPTIMIZING YOUR DAILY SCHEDULE   1
   Mapping Your Day for Maximum Efficiency   1
   The Role of Breaks and Downtime   2
   Mastering the Art of Saying No   3
   Time Blocking for Focused Work   5
   Leveraging Technology for Time Optimization   6
   Adapting to Unplanned Changes   7
   Creating a Supportive Environment   8

2. HARNESSING TIME FOR CREATIVITY AND
   INNOVATION   9
   Fostering Creative Thinking   9
   Managing Time for Innovative Projects   11
   The Role of Reflection in Creativity   12
   Time Management in Team Creativity   13
   Balancing Urgent and Important Tasks   14
   Creating Space for Deep Work   16
   Leveraging Downtime for Creative Insights   17

3. TIME MANAGEMENT FOR PERSONAL
   DEVELOPMENT   19
   Setting Personal Development Goals   19
   Allocating Time for Learning and Growth   21
   The Role of Mentorship and Coaching   22
   Leveraging Resources for Self-Improvement   23
   Overcoming Plateaus and Stagnation   25
   Integrating New Skills and Knowledge   26
   Reflecting and Adjusting Personal
   Development Plans   27

4. BUILDING RESILIENCE AND FLEXIBILITY 29
   Understanding Resilience in Time
   Management 29
   Adapting to Changing Circumstances 31
   Developing a Growth Mindset 32
   Managing Stress and Burnout 33
   The Power of Positive Habits 34
   Embracing Uncertainty and Risk 35
   Cultivating Emotional Intelligence 36

5. EFFECTIVE COMMUNICATION AND TIME
   MANAGEMENT 39
   Mastering Time-Saving Communication Skills 39
   Managing Time in Meetings and
   Collaborations 41
   Setting Expectations and Boundaries 42
   Leveraging Technology for Effective
   Communication 43
   Dealing with Communication Overload 44
   Cultivating Conciseness and Clarity 45
   Feedback: Giving and Receiving 46

6. LEVERAGING TIME FOR HEALTH AND
   WELLNESS 49
   Balancing Health with Busy Schedules 49
   Exercise and Time Management 51
   Nutrition and Time 52
   Mindfulness and Meditation 53
   Sleep and Productivity 54
   Stress Management Techniques 56
   Holistic Wellness Approaches 57

7. STRATEGIC PLANNING AND GOAL
   SETTING 59
   Crafting Effective Long-Term Plans 59
   Setting and Achieving SMART Goals 61
   The Role of Vision in Planning 62
   Breaking Down Goals into Manageable Steps 63
   Planning for Contingencies 64
   Aligning Goals with Personal Values 65
   Regular Review and Adjustment of Plans 66

8. OPTIMIZING WORK ENVIRONMENTS   68
Creating Productive Workspaces   68
Leveraging Technology Wisely   70
Time Management in Remote and
Hybrid Work   71
Building a Supportive Team Culture   72
Navigating Office Politics and Time Wasters   73
Integrating Work and Personal Life   74
Evolving with Changing Work Trends   75

9. TIME MANAGEMENT FOR CREATIVES   77
Fostering Creativity Within Time Constraints   77
Managing Time in Creative Projects   78
Overcoming Creative Blocks   80
Time Management in Artistic Professions   81
Leveraging Collaboration and Networking   82
Integrating New Technologies   83
Sustaining a Long-term Creative Career   84

10. TIME MANAGEMENT FOR
ENTREPRENEURS   86
Prioritizing in a Startup Environment   86
Balancing Innovation and Execution   87
Effective Delegation and Leadership   89
Time Management in Scaling Businesses   90
Networking and Relationship Building   91
Risk Management and Time Allocation   92
Sustaining Personal Well-being   93

11. TIME MANAGEMENT FOR STUDENTS   95
Balancing Academics, Work, and Social Life   95
Effective Study Techniques   96
Managing Time for Exams and Deadlines   98
Time Management in Extracurricular
Activities   99
Planning for Future Careers and Goals   100
Leveraging Technology for Academic
Efficiency   101
Building Support Networks   102

12. TIME MANAGEMENT FOR PARENTS 104
Balancing Parenting and Personal Time 104
Effective Routines for Families 105
Managing Time for Children's Activities 107
Parenting in the Digital Age 108
Self-Care for Parents 109
Educating Children on Time Management 110
Family Planning and Future Goals 111

13. ADVANCED TIME MANAGEMENT
TECHNIQUES 113
Mastering Time Management Tools and Apps 114
Optimizing Workflows for Peak Efficiency 115
The Psychology of Procrastination and
Overcoming It 116
Time Management in High-Pressure
Environments 117
Integrating Time Management with Life Goals 118
Continuous Improvement and Adaptation 119
Beyond Time Management: A Holistic
Approach 120

14. THE FUTURE OF TIME MANAGEMENT 122
Emerging Trends in Time Management 122
Integrating Time Management with
Sustainable Living 124
The Role of AI and Automation 125
Time Management for Lifelong Learning 126
Global Perspectives on Time Management 127
Personal and Professional Harmony 128
Visioning the Future of Work and Life 129

*Conclusion: Consolidating Time Mastery for a
Fulfilling Life* 131
Appendix 1: The Pomodoro Method 141
Appendix 2: The Eisenhower Matrix 145

PREFACE

REDEFINING TIME MANAGEMENT

Time management, often confined to task organization and scheduling, stands on the cusp of a profound transformation. This book introduces a revolutionary perspective, painting time management as a quest for efficiency and a journey of making meaningful choices that mirror our deepest values and dreams. It's an invitation to see time not just as a sequence of intervals to be allocated but as the vibrant backdrop against which the story of our lives is painted.

This reimagined concept shifts the emphasis from the quantity of tasks to the quality and fulfillment they bring. It's a philosophy that advocates for harmony that fosters accomplishment without compromising personal well-being. This narrative emphasizes the importance of using our time wisely and making choices that are in line with our long-term goals rather than letting the tide of immediate obligations sweep us away.

Within this new framework, time management is envisioned as an all-encompassing practice intricately woven into every facet of life. It's about recognizing the delicate dance between different areas of our existence—work, family, personal development, and leisure—and striking a chord of balance among them. This book serves as a compass for navigating this comprehensive approach, leading the way to a more balanced and enriching engagement with time.

FROM TIME WASTERS TO TIME SAVERS

Addressing and curtailing time wasters is an essential step in mastering time management. This book delves into the ubiquitous traps that siphon our time, ranging from unchecked digital indulgences to the snares of procrastination, and offers actionable strategies to counteract them. It's about pinpointing the habitual patterns that squander time and consciously reshaping them into more fruitful and productive behaviors.

The shift from habits that dissipate time to those that conserve it requires awareness and the embrace of new, beneficial routines. This section is replete with hands-on advice for cultivating practices and systems that conserve time and amplify productivity. It encompasses guidance on a spectrum of tactics, from tidying up workspaces to refining decision-making processes.

A pivotal aspect of time conservation is mastering the art of declining non-essential tasks and distractions. This book ventures into the nuanced art of establishing boundaries and selecting tasks that resonate with one's personal and professional objectives. It's about finding clarity in what's truly significant and mustering the resolve to prioritize those facets, even if it entails relinquishing less critical commitments.

THE JOURNEY TO TIME MASTERY

The journey to time mastery is a personal and ongoing process. This book provides insights on how to transform one's relationships with time, showcasing the diverse paths to mastering this skill. These insights provide both motivation and helpful applications for the journey.

Time management lessons are woven throughout this journey, providing a blend of theory and practice. The book distills critical insights and offers a wide variety of ideas and strategies that readers can adapt to their own lives. These lessons are practical, insightful, and grounded in real-world experience.

Central to this journey is the development of habits that support effective time management. This book explores the psychology behind habit formation and offers guidance on building routines that enhance productivity and well-being. It's about creating habits that are sustainable, enjoyable, and aligned with personal values.

THE CORE PRINCIPLES OF THIS APPROACH

At the heart of this time management methodology lie the fundamental principles of balance, intentionality, and adaptability. This book lays the groundwork for these foundational concepts, paving the way for unfolding strategies and techniques. It's centered on grasping the core philosophy that anchors effective time management, priming the reader for its practical implementation.

Embracing a holistic perspective on time is a crucial principle of this approach. It involves viewing time management as a standalone task and an integral component of overall life management, impacting every facet of existence. This principle champions a balanced rhythm of life where productivity is seamlessly intertwined with personal wellness.

Another central tenet underscored in this book is the significance of reflection and adaptability. It accentuates the necessity for continual self-evaluation and the agility to modify time management tactics as needed. It's about maintaining an openness to evolution, drawing lessons from lived experiences, and perpetually honing one's time management style.

TOOLS AND TECHNIQUES FOR A NEW AGE

In this segment, we navigate through a curated selection of tools and tactics crafted for the nuanced demands of contemporary living. It spans an array of approaches, from cutting-edge digital applications that boost efficiency to classic techniques such as the Pomodoro method. The emphasis lies in assembling a versatile toolkit that readers can tailor to their personal requirements and life scenarios.

Navigating the convergence of technology and time constitutes a pivotal element of current time management paradigms. This book navigates the intricacies of utilizing technology to its fullest potential, sidestepping its traps while capitalizing on its capacity to streamline processes and elevate productivity. It provides a compass for selecting and employing digital resources in a manner that amplifies, rather than impedes, proficient time management.

The personalization of tools and methodologies is a recurring theme in this section. It acknowledges the diversity of individual needs, advocating for a bespoke approach to time management. The narrative empowers readers to mold these tools and techniques to align with their distinct rhythms, tastes, and aspirations.

EMBRACING A MINDFUL APPROACH TO TIME

A mindful approach to time involves being present and intentional with how we spend our hours and minutes. This book delves into the concept of mindfulness in the context of time management, exploring how being fully engaged in the present moment can enhance productivity and satisfaction. It includes practical tips on incorporating mindfulness into daily routines, enabling a deeper and more meaningful engagement with time.

The power of presence in productivity is a crucial theme in this section. It's about the benefits of focusing intensely on the task at hand, minimizing distractions, and fully immersing oneself in the moment. This focus leads to higher-quality work, greater enjoyment, and a sense of fulfillment.

Strategies for mindful time use are provided, offering readers ways to practice mindfulness in their daily lives. These strategies involve conscious decision-making about how to spend time and prioritizing activities that align with personal values and goals. It's about making each moment count, whether at work or leisure.

SETTING THE FOUNDATION FOR SUCCESS

At the heart of mastering time management lies the art of crafting and pursuing goals that resonate with one's deepest aspirations and values. This book leads readers through the journey of establishing clear, achievable, and meaningful objectives, underscoring the significance of ensuring these goals harmonize with personal ideals and desires, thus making the quest both fulfilling and intentional.

Creating a customized time management blueprint is vital for realizing these goals. This segment presents a detailed roadmap for devising such a plan that is attuned to individual preferences and situations. It encompasses practical advice on sorting tasks by priority, setting attainable timelines, and shaping systems and routines that bolster the attainment of set goals.

Establishing a conducive environment for this transformative journey forms the final cornerstone of the foundation. The discussion here extends beyond mere physical organization to the creation of a supportive social and emotional milieu. It encompasses strategies for arranging physical spaces efficiently, nurturing relationships that bolster time management efforts, and fostering a culture that values and respects time. This nurturing backdrop is pivotal for the successful implementation and longevity of effective time management practices.

Moreover, this supportive environment transcends the tangible and encompasses the social and emotional facets of our lives. The narrative highlights the importance of being surrounded by people who appreciate and support your time management ambitions, be they family, friends, or colleagues. A network that encourages and assists you on this path can be instrumental in successfully integrating these strategies into your life.

The book also delves into the psychological readiness for change, offering insights into surmounting resistance and adopting new habits. It's about cultivating a mindset that views change as a gateway to personal growth and improvement, rather than a hurdle.

Flexibility and responsiveness to life's shifts form another critical element of this foundation. The book offers tactics for adjusting your time management plan as life evolves, ensuring its relevance and effectiveness over time.

Understanding and overcoming personal impediments to effective time use is another focus. The book addresses common challenges like procrastination and fear of failure, offering concrete strategies to navigate past these barriers.

Learning to balance immediate needs with long-term ambitions is also explored. This guide helps readers align daily actions with broader life goals, ensuring each day contributes meaningfully towards long-term aspirations.

Lastly, the book champions continuous learning as a cornerstone of successful time management. It encourages readers to see time management as an evolving skill, highlighting the value of lifelong learning and openness to new knowledge and strategies.

In sum, this book outlines a multi-dimensional approach to time management, intertwining goal setting, personalized planning, a supportive environment, adaptability, overcoming personal challenges, balancing short-term and long-term goals, and a commitment to ongoing learning. It equips readers with the tools and insights to build a solid foundation, steering them towards a more organized, productive, and enriching time management journey.

INTRODUCTION

UNDERSTANDING TIME'S TRUE VALUE

The relentless march of time and its irreplaceable nature elevates it to our most valued asset. Grasping the true essence of time starts with a personal evaluation of our daily conduct. We unravel the fabric of our time use by contemplating our everyday habits and decisions. This self-examination sheds light on areas where our investment of time is fruitful and those where our choices could be more impactful.

Understanding the value of time also means coming to terms with its non-recoverable nature. Time stands apart from other resources in its inability to be hoarded or regained. Once a moment slips by, it's lost in the annals of history. This understanding spurs us to deliberate more carefully on our time use, giving precedence to activities that resonate with our core values and aspirations.

The principle of opportunity cost is pivotal in appreciating time's worth. Every decision on how to utilize time carries the cost of alternative options not taken. Grasping this idea steers us toward making decisions that yield the greatest personal and professional satisfaction and success.

Ultimately, grasping the true value of time transcends mere acknowledgment of its scarcity; it involves realizing its immense potential. It's about making deliberate choices that convert time from a vanishing resource into a driving force for substantial experiences and accomplishments.

PRIORITIZING FOR IMPACT

Prioritizing for impact is crucial to mastering time management. This section explores the art of discerning what is truly important and focusing efforts on those areas. It involves identifying tasks that demand immediate attention and understanding which activities will have the most significant long-term impact.

Effective prioritization begins with precise goal-setting. By defining what we aim to achieve in various facets of our lives, we can align our daily tasks with these broader objectives. This alignment ensures that our daily actions are not just busy work but steps towards meaningful achievements.

Tools and techniques for prioritization are diverse and varied. This section introduces practical methods for identifying and focusing on key priorities, from traditional to-do lists to more advanced decision-making frameworks. These tools help sort through the myriad of tasks and responsibilities we face, highlighting those that deserve our focus.

The challenge of prioritizing in a world filled with distractions and competing demands is addressed. This includes strategies for maintaining focus on priorities, even in the face of urgent but less important tasks. It's about learning to distinguish between true priorities and distractions masquerading as immediate necessities.

THE POWER OF FOCUS

Time management, often perceived as a mere set of organizational tactics, is on the cusp of a transformative reevaluation. This book introduces a groundbreaking perspective, envisioning time management as a journey beyond mere efficiency. It's a journey towards making impactful decisions that resonate with our deepest values and dreams, recognizing that time isn't just a sequence of intervals to be allocated but rather a rich tapestry upon which the narrative of our lives is etched.

This reimagined approach shifts the emphasis from the sheer volume of completed tasks to the quality and fulfillment they bring. It advocates for a balance where achievement coexists with well-being, urging us to be deliberate in how we utilize our time. This means aligning our actions with our long-term aspirations, not just the pressing demands of the moment.

Adopting this holistic perspective, time management becomes an integrated aspect of our entire existence. It's a delicate balance, harmonizing the different facets of our lives —work, family, personal development, and leisure. This book serves as a guide, leading readers through a holistic strategy that enables a more enriching and balanced allocation of time.

BALANCING TIME ACROSS LIFE'S DOMAINS

Uncovering and addressing time wasters is an essential component of refining time management. This book dives into the various traps that can consume our time, ranging from unchecked digital usage to the habit of procrastination. It's about discerning the habits that lead to inefficient use of time and intentionally replacing them with practices that enhance productivity.

The shift from habits that waste time to those that optimize it is more than just being aware; it involves cultivating new, more productive habits. This part of the book offers actionable advice on building routines and systems to economize time and boost efficiency. The guidance spans a range of practices, including how to effectively organize workspaces and streamline the decision-making process.

One of the fundamental strategies for conserving time is mastering the ability to decline non-critical tasks and distractions. This book explores the nuances of establishing boundaries and focusing on tasks that align with one's personal and professional objectives. It emphasizes the importance of identifying what's truly significant and summoning the resolve to concentrate on these priorities, even at the expense of less important activities.

TIME MANAGEMENT FOR LONG-TERM GOALS

At the heart of this time management methodology lie the fundamental tenets of balance, intentionality, and adaptability. This book delineates these fundamental principles, laying a robust groundwork for the array of strategies and techniques that are elaborated upon later. It delves into the core philosophy underpinning effective time management, preparing the reader for its practical application.

Central to this approach is a holistic perspective on time. This viewpoint treats time management not as an isolated skill but as an integral component of overall life management, acknowledging its influence on every aspect of one's life. This principle champions a well-rounded approach, striving for harmony between achieving productivity and nurturing personal well-being.

Another pivotal principle is the significance of reflection and the ability to adapt. The book underscores the importance of regular self-review and the adaptability of time management approaches. It encourages an openness to evolution, a willingness to learn from various experiences, and an ongoing process of refining and enhancing one's time management techniques.

THE ART OF DELEGATION AND COLLABORATION

Delegation and collaboration are critical aspects of effective time management, particularly in professional contexts. This section explores the importance of delegating tasks and collaborating with others to maximize time efficiency and productivity. It emphasizes that effective delegation is not abdicating responsibility but rather strategically allocating resources.

Tools and strategies for effective delegation are presented. This includes identifying tasks suitable for delegation, selecting the right people for these tasks, and communicating expectations clearly. The goal is to ensure that delegation leads to enhanced productivity and allows for a focus on higher-level tasks.

The role of collaboration in time management is examined. Collaborative efforts can lead to more efficient use of time, pooling of skills, and greater impact. This section provides tips for building and nurturing collaborative relationships and creating environments where teamwork thrives.

Overcoming challenges in delegation and collaboration is also addressed. This includes dealing with reluctance to delegate, managing different work styles, and ensuring clear and effective communication among team members. Strategies for overcoming these challenges are provided, ensuring that delegation and collaboration contribute positively to time management efforts.

HARNESSING THE POWER OF ROUTINES

The establishment and maintenance of effective routines are fundamental to time mastery. This section delves into the benefits of routines, including increased efficiency, reduced decision fatigue, and the creation of a stable framework for daily activities. It discusses how routines can provide structure and predictability, enhancing time management.

Strategies for developing and maintaining effective routines are explored. This includes tips for creating routines that align with personal and professional goals, are flexible enough to accommodate changes, and are sustainable over the long term. The aim is to develop routines that support productivity and well-being.

The role of habits in reinforcing routines is examined. Habits, both good and bad, play a significant role in how routines are established and maintained. This section offers insights into habit formation and change, providing readers with tools to build habits that support their routines and time management goals.

Adapting routines to changing circumstances is also addressed. Life is dynamic, and routines must be flexible enough to adapt to new situations. This section discusses how to adjust routines to respond to life changes, ensuring they continue serving their purpose effectively.

OPTIMIZING YOUR DAILY SCHEDULE

*R*efining your daily schedule is a pivotal element in mastering time management. This process transcends the mere allocation of tasks throughout the day. It's about engaging in deliberate planning, acknowledging the necessity of a balanced approach, and employing tools and techniques that elevate your productivity. This chapter delves into the multifaceted nature of optimizing your daily itinerary, covering everything from skillful planning of your day to gracefully adapting to unforeseen shifts.

MAPPING YOUR DAY FOR MAXIMUM EFFICIENCY

The first step in optimizing your daily schedule is mapping out your day with a focus on efficiency. This involves not just listing tasks but strategically planning when and how to tackle them. It requires an understanding of one's own productivity rhythms and aligning tasks with these peak times. Effective day mapping also means being realistic about what can be achieved in a day and setting achievable goals that motivate rather than overwhelm.

In mapping out the day, it's crucial to identify priorities. This means distinguishing between tasks that are urgent and important and those that can wait. By focusing on priorities, you ensure that your energy is spent on activities that have the greatest impact. This process involves daily reflection and adjustment, as priorities can shift over time.

Allocating specific time slots to tasks can increase efficiency. This involves estimating how much time each task will take and fitting it into your schedule accordingly. It's a balancing act—ensuring that there's enough time for each task while also being flexible enough to accommodate any overruns or unexpected demands.

The mapping process also includes scheduling time for unexpected tasks and interruptions. While it's important to have a structured plan, it's equally important to be flexible. Allocating buffer time within your schedule can help absorb the impact of unforeseen events without derailing your entire day.

Regular review and adjustment of your daily map are essential. As you go through your day, note what works and what doesn't. This continuous improvement process helps refine your scheduling skills, making you more adept at planning and executing your daily tasks.

THE ROLE OF BREAKS AND DOWNTIME

In an efficiently managed schedule, breaks and downtime are not mere interludes but essential elements that sustain high productivity levels. Rather than being mere pauses in the workflow, they are critical for reenergizing the mind, alleviating stress, and averting burnout. Breaks can spark creativity, bolster mental well-being, and heighten job satis-faction.

Incorporating breaks into your day with strategic intent can optimize their positive impact. Short, consistent breaks typi-cally yield better results than infrequent, extended ones. Methods such as the Pomodoro Technique (see Appendix 1), which alternates focused work sessions with brief rest peri-ods, are beneficial for maintaining concentration and vigor.

Downtime, encompassing more extended rest periods like evenings and weekends, is vital for long-term well-being. These stretches, devoid of work obligations, are crucial for mental and physical rejuvenation and open up space for leisure pursuits that bring joy and relaxation.

The effectiveness of breaks and downtime hinges as much on their quality as on their frequency. The goal isn't just to step away from work but to engage in activities that genuinely revitalize and refresh you. Whether it's a stroll, a cherished hobby, or simply basking in tranquility, the crux lies in finding pursuits that offer a true respite from work.

Discipline is vital in scheduling and committing to breaks and downtime. Amidst the whirlwind of a busy day, it's tempting to bypass breaks under the guise of productivity. This approach, however, can be detrimental in the long term. Setting regular reminders or adhering to a fixed break schedule can help ensure these crucial pauses are observed regularly.

MASTERING THE ART OF SAYING NO

Developing the ability to say no is critical to effective time management. It's about establishing clear boundaries and safeguarding your time from unwarranted intrusions. Becoming adept at this skill means acknowledging that you can't undertake every task and that overextending yourself can lead to stress and even burnout.

The journey to comfortably saying no begins with a firm grasp of your priorities and objectives. With a clear understanding of what matters most to you, it becomes simpler to turn down requests or opportunities that don't align with these goals. It's a process of making deliberate decisions that bolster your overarching aspirations.

Effective communication is integral to saying no. It's not merely about rejecting offers but about doing so in a manner that is both respectful and unambiguous. This involves articulating your reasons, suggesting feasible alternatives, and balancing firmness and courtesy in your responses.

Confronting and overcoming the guilt often associated with saying no is vital. Many grapple with the worry of letting others down or missing out. Yet, it's crucial to remember that declining one option often means embracing another—typically, one that's more aligned with your essential needs and goals.

You can practice and refine the art of saying no through incremental steps. Begin by saying no in less pivotal situations and gradually build the confidence to apply it in more consequential instances. Each instance of saying no is a step towards enhanced time management and achieving a more harmonious balance in life.

TIME BLOCKING FOR FOCUSED WORK

Time blocking is a powerful technique for optimizing your daily schedule. It involves dedicating specific blocks of time to particular tasks or activities. This method helps create a structure for your day, ensuring that important tasks get the dedicated time they deserve.

The effectiveness of time blocking lies in its ability to help you focus. You are less likely to become distracted by other tasks or interruptions if you set aside a specific time for a task. It creates a sense of urgency and purpose, helping you stay focused on the task at hand.

Time blocking also aids in task batching. This involves grouping and handling similar tasks in a single time block. Batching can increase efficiency by reducing the time lost in task switching and helping maintain a consistent focus.

To implement time blocking effectively, start by identifying the tasks that need to be done and estimating how much time each will take. Then, create blocks of time in your schedule for these tasks, considering your natural energy levels and productivity rhythms throughout the day.

Flexibility is critical in time-blocking. While it's important to stick to your schedule, be prepared to adjust your blocks as needed. Unexpected tasks or changes in priorities can necessitate shifts in your schedule, and being adaptable is crucial for effective time management.

LEVERAGING TECHNOLOGY FOR TIME OPTIMIZATION

Technology stands as a formidable partner in refining your daily schedule. It brings to the table many options, from sophisticated calendar applications to comprehensive task management systems designed to streamline your time management. Yet, the key lies in the astute utilization of these technological tools to ensure they bolster rather than impede your productivity.

Selecting the most suitable technological aids is a critical step. Aim for tools that resonate with your unique require-ments and work habits. Whether you need an all-encom-passing project management solution or a straightforward to-do list application, the primary objective is to choose tools that aid in organizing, prioritizing, and monitoring your tasks efficiently.

Harnessing technology for automating routine activities can lead to substantial time savings. Automation tools are adept at managing everyday tasks like filtering emails, scheduling appointments, or managing social media posts, thereby liberating your time for more significant endeavors.

Moreover, technology serves as an enabler for seamless communication and teamwork. With tools like video confer-encing software, instant messaging apps, and collaborative platforms, you can streamline your communication processes, enhancing efficiency and reducing the need for lengthy and often unproductive meetings.

However, staying vigilant about technology's propensity to distract is imperative. Exercise caution to avoid excessive immersion in digital tools or letting constant notifications fracture your concentration. Establishing clear boundaries and employing technology with purpose and intent is crucial to fully harnessing its potential for optimizing your time.

ADAPTING TO UNPLANNED CHANGES

Even with meticulous planning, your day can often take unexpected turns. Adapting to these unforeseen changes is vital to time management, calling for flexibility, resilience, and ingenuity in responding to disruptions.

When unforeseen shifts occur, the initial step is to evaluate how they affect your agenda. Decide which tasks can be delayed, which demand immediate attention, and which can be passed on to others. It's about swiftly yet judiciously rearranging your priorities to accommodate these new developments.

Crafting a backup plan for essential tasks is an effective strategy to lessen the impact of sudden changes. This might mean setting earlier deadlines for critical projects or having alternative plans for important meetings. Being equipped for potential interruptions can ease the stress of adapting to them.

Embracing a positive mindset when faced with change is essential. Rather than seeing disruptions as hindrances, view them as chances to showcase your flexibility and problem-solving capabilities. This optimistic outlook can greatly aid in smoothly navigating through unexpected changes.

Each encounter with unplanned change is an opportunity to sharpen your adaptability. Reflect on your responses' efficacy and learn from successes and shortcomings. These reflections will help refine your strategies for managing disruptions, steadily enhancing your prowess in dealing with life's unpredictable elements.

CREATING A SUPPORTIVE ENVIRONMENT

Creating a conducive environment is a cornerstone of effective time management. This involves organizing your physical space and nurturing a supportive social and emotional atmosphere.

Ensuring your physical workspace is optimized for productivity is crucial. This means maintaining a tidy, well-organized area equipped with the necessary tools and resources. An orderly workspace minimizes distractions and aids in concentrating on your tasks.

The social aspect of your environment is equally influential in time management. It's important to surround yourself with people who respect and support your time management goals. Be it family, friends, or colleagues, a network that understands your goals can significantly enhance your ability to manage your time efficiently.

Establishing clear boundaries is fundamental to creating this supportive environment. This could involve defining specific work hours, communicating your availability to others, or setting guidelines around interruptions. Clear boundaries help others understand and respect your time management requirements.

Practicing self-compassion is also crucial. Accept that achieving perfection in time management is unrealistic, and expect days when plans may falter. Treat yourself kindly during these times, viewing them as chances for learning and growth.

HARNESSING TIME FOR CREATIVITY AND INNOVATION

Effectively managing time transcends mere productivity; it's a catalyst for sparking creativity and driving innovation. This chapter dives into how adept time management can carve out room for creative thought, facilitate the realization of inventive projects, and nurture an atmosphere conducive to creative flourishing.

FOSTERING CREATIVE THINKING

Creativity often flourishes when time is treated as a canvas rather than a constraint. Fostering creative thinking starts with allowing time for exploration and free thought. It means scheduling periods where the mind is encouraged to wander, question, and dream without the pressure of immediate outcomes.

Balancing structured and unstructured time is critical to fostering creativity. While structure brings discipline, unstructured time brings freedom—the freedom to explore ideas without boundaries. You can achieve this balance by alternating periods of focused work with unstructured time slots for brainstorming and free association.

The environment also plays a crucial role in fostering creativity. Spaces that inspire and stimulate the mind can contribute significantly to creative thinking. Whether it's a physical space designed for brainstorming or a virtual space that encourages collaboration, the right environment can enhance creative processes.

Encouraging a culture of curiosity and continuous learning can also stimulate creative thinking. This involves promoting a mindset where questioning and exploring are valued and learning is seen as an ongoing journey, not a destination. In such a culture, time spent learning and exploring new ideas is seen as an investment in creativity.

Diversity of thought and experience can significantly boost creativity. Bringing together people from different back-grounds and disciplines can create a fusion of ideas, perspec-tives, and solutions. Allocating time for cross-functional collaboration and idea exchange can be a powerful catalyst for creative thinking.

Rest and relaxation should not be underestimated in their ability to foster creativity. Sometimes, stepping away from a problem or project can provide the mental space for creative insights to surface. This restorative time can be as important as active working time in the creative process.

Creativity often emerges from the intersection of different ideas and disciplines. Encouraging team members to explore areas outside their expertise and to bring diverse insights into their work can lead to unexpected and innovative solutions. Time spent exploring these intersections can be incredibly fruitful for creativity.

MANAGING TIME FOR INNOVATIVE PROJECTS

Innovative projects often require a different time management approach than routine tasks. These projects, by their nature, involve exploration, experimentation, and a degree of uncertainty. Managing time effectively in this context means being flexible and adaptable.

Setting realistic timelines is critical for innovative projects. These timelines should account for the exploratory nature of the work, allowing for iteration and refinement. This might mean building in extra time for research, experimentation, and unforeseen challenges.

Prioritizing tasks within innovative projects is essential. This involves identifying which aspects of the project are critical to its success and focusing time and resources on these elements. It also means letting go of or delaying less critical tasks.

Regular check-ins and milestones can keep innovative projects on track. These checkpoints provide opportunities to assess progress, make adjustments, and realign with the project's goals. They can also serve as motivational milestones, marking achievements along the journey.

Innovative projects often benefit from bursts of intense focus followed by periods of reflection. This pattern enables in-depth work on complex problems, then time to take a step back and evaluate the work from a wider perspective. Managing time to allow for these cycles can enhance the quality and impact of the work.

Encouraging a risk-taking mindset is essential to managing time for innovation. This means allocating time for exploring untested ideas and approaches, even if they carry a risk of failure. A culture that embraces calculated risks can lead to breakthrough innovations.

Documentation and reflection throughout the project can save time in the long run. Keeping records of processes, decisions, and learnings provides a valuable reference for the current project and future endeavors. It helps build a knowledge base that can streamline future projects and foster continuous improvement.

THE ROLE OF REFLECTION IN CREATIVITY

Reflection stands as a cornerstone in the realm of creativity, offering a pause from the immediate to contemplate the larger picture, forge connections among ideas, and gauge progress. Dedicating moments for reflection can unearth profound insights and pave the way for more groundbreaking solutions.

The practice of reflection can manifest in various forms, ranging from structured reviews and debriefs to more casual methods like journaling or meditative exercises. The essence lies in carving out a mental sanctuary for thought and synthesis, free from the immediacy of action.

Collective reflection sessions, such as brainstorming gatherings or post-project analyses, bring together a wealth of perspectives and collaborative thoughts. These interactions can become fertile grounds for innovation, enhancing the communal creative journey.

Personal reflection holds equal significance. It offers a conduit to one's deepest thoughts and ideas, often birthing distinctive and groundbreaking concepts. Investing time in personal contemplation can yield substantial dividends in the creative process.

Rather than being an afterthought, reflection should be a continual practice woven throughout the lifespan of a project. Regular reflective pauses provide ongoing feedback and guidance, ensuring the creative journey stays aligned and purposeful.

Cultivating a reflective culture within teams and organizations encourages a deeper, more innovative approach to projects. This culture places a premium on reflective practices, integrating them into the regular ebb and flow of work.

True reflection also involves embracing feedback and learning from every outcome, whether a triumph or a setback. Such openness cultivates a mindset of growth, where each experience is viewed as a stepping stone for learning and evolving.

TIME MANAGEMENT IN TEAM CREATIVITY

Managing time effectively in a team setting is crucial for fostering creativity. It involves coordinating the efforts of multiple individuals, each with their own schedules and working styles, towards a common creative goal.

Establishing clear goals and expectations for the team helps in aligning efforts and managing time efficiently. This clarity ensures that everyone understands their role and how their work contributes to the overall project.

Effective communication is crucial to time management in team creativity. Regular check-ins, clear communication channels, and transparent sharing of information help keep the team aligned and on track.

Balancing individual work with collaborative sessions can enhance team creativity. While individual work allows for a focused effort on specific tasks, collaborative sessions can bring together diverse ideas and perspectives.

Recognizing and accommodating different working styles within the team is important. This might involve allowing flexibility in work hours or providing different environments for focused work and collaborative sessions.

Time management tools and technology can aid in coordinating team efforts. From shared calendars to project management software, these tools can help keep the team organized and ensure everyone knows deadlines and milestones.

Celebrating milestones and achievements can be a powerful motivator for team creativity. Recognizing progress and successes, no matter how small, can boost morale and keep the team motivated toward their creative goals.

BALANCING URGENT AND IMPORTANT TASKS

The distinction between urgent and important tasks is crucial in the realm of creativity and innovation. Urgent tasks demand immediate attention but are not necessarily aligned with long-term goals. Important tasks, while not always pressing, are critical to achieving long-term objectives.

The Eisenhower Matrix (see Appendix 2) is a useful tool for categorizing tasks into urgent, important, both, or neither. This categorization helps in prioritizing tasks and allocating time effectively.

Focusing on important tasks requires discipline and foresight. It involves resisting the temptation to constantly address urgent but less impactful tasks and instead dedicating time to activities that contribute to long-term goals.

Balancing urgent and important tasks often involves setting boundaries and managing expectations. This might mean communicating availability, delegating urgent tasks, or setting aside dedicated time for important work.

Prioritizing important tasks can also involve saying no to new commitments or requests that do not align with long-term objectives. This selective approach ensures that time and resources are focused on activities that truly matter.

Regularly reviewing and adjusting priorities is essential. As circumstances change, what was once important may become less so, and vice versa. Staying flexible and responsive to these changes ensures that time is always aligned with current priorities.

Time management techniques such as time blocking can effectively balance urgent and important tasks. By allocating specific blocks of time for important work, you can ensure that these tasks receive the attention they deserve, even amidst urgent demands.

CREATING SPACE FOR DEEP WORK

Deep work—the ability to focus intensely on cognitively demanding tasks—is crucial for creativity and innovation. Creating space for deep work involves setting aside dedicated, uninterrupted time for a focused effort on complex tasks.

Minimizing distractions is essential for deep work. This involves creating an environment conducive to concentration, whether it's a quiet physical space or a digital environment free from notifications and interruptions.

Establishing routines and rituals can help transition into a state of deep work. Whether it's a specific start time, a particular workspace, or a pre-work ritual, these routines signal to the brain that it's time to focus.

Setting clear goals for each deep work session helps maintain focus and direction. Knowing what you aim to achieve in the session provides a roadmap for your effort and keeps you on track.

Limiting the length of deep work sessions can prevent burnout and maintain quality. Working in intense bursts followed by breaks allows for sustained concentration without diminishing returns.

Incorporating deep work into your daily or weekly schedule requires planning and commitment. It involves prioritizing and protecting these sessions from other demands on your time.

Reflecting on and adjusting your approach to deep work can enhance its effectiveness. Paying attention to what works and what doesn't allows you to refine your deep work practices for greater productivity and satisfaction.

LEVERAGING DOWNTIME FOR CREATIVE INSIGHTS

Downtime, often overlooked, can be fertile ground for creative insights. Allowing the mind to rest and wander can lead to unexpected connections and ideas. Scheduled downtime, such as regular breaks or days off, provides an opportunity for the subconscious mind to process and synthesize information. During these periods, ideas that have been simmering in the background can come to the forefront.

Engaging in activities unrelated to work during downtime can stimulate creativity. Activities like hobbies, reading, or even casual conversations can provide new perspectives and spark creative ideas. These activities encourage the mind to make novel connections and explore different viewpoints.

Mindfulness and relaxation techniques can also enhance creativity during downtime. Practices such as meditation, deep breathing, or simply being in nature can clear the mind, reduce stress, and open up space for creative thoughts to emerge.

Reflecting during downtime, rather than actively trying to solve problems, can lead to breakthrough ideas. This passive reflection allows the brain to work in the background, connecting dots and generating solutions in a relaxed state.

Encouraging a culture that values downtime is important for team creativity. Recognizing that rest and relaxation can contribute to creative insights encourages team members to take the time they need to recharge and return to work with fresh ideas.

Balancing active work with adequate downtime is vital to maintaining long-term creativity. While hard work and focused effort are important, they should be complemented with periods of rest to prevent burnout and sustain creative energy.

Downtime should not be seen as time wasted but as an essential component of the creative process. By strategically leveraging downtime for relaxation, reflection, and unrelated activities, individuals and teams can enhance their creative potential and generate innovative ideas and solutions.

TIME MANAGEMENT FOR PERSONAL DEVELOPMENT

*W*ithin the sphere of personal growth, mastering time management transcends mere efficiency—it's a journey toward deliberate self-enhancement and growth. This chapter explores an array of strategies designed to aid in establishing and realizing personal development objectives. It covers carving out time for educational pursuits, the value of mentorship and coaching, utilizing available resources effectively, breaking through periods of stagnation, assimilating new abilities, and consistently reevaluating and fine-tuning personal development strategies.

SETTING PERSONAL DEVELOPMENT GOALS

Establishing personal development goals is a fundamental step in the journey of self-improvement. This process starts with deep self-reflection on one's ambitions, strengths, and areas needing growth. Effective goals must be specific, measurable, achievable, relevant, and time-bound (SMART).

These goals act as beacons, providing direction and infusing a sense of purpose.

Striking a balance between ambition and practicality is vital to setting these goals. While it's important to stretch your boundaries, overly ambitious goals can lead to frustration and a loss of motivation. A balanced approach involves challenging yourself within the realm of your current abilities and life situation.

The power of visualization in achieving personal development goals cannot be overstated. Picturing the desired outcome and its accompanying rewards not only crafts a mental image of success but also helps keep your focus and drive alive.

Ensuring that your personal development goals align with your fundamental values is crucial. Goals that resonate deeply with your beliefs and principles are pursued with more vigor and commitment, leading to a more fulfilling journey and satisfying results.

Breaking down larger goals into smaller, more manageable steps can simplify the process and make it more achievable. This strategy allows for celebrating incremental victories and maintaining your drive and momentum throughout the journey.

Adaptability in setting goals is also crucial. As individuals grow and change, their goals may also need to evolve. Staying open to modifying your goals in light of new experiences and insights ensures that your personal development remains pertinent and in sync with your evolving self.

A commitment to regularly reviewing and reassessing your goals is imperative. This process entails monitoring progress, identifying any obstacles, and making adjustments as needed to stay on course. Regular reviews help keep your goals front and center in your mind, ensuring steady progress toward achieving them.

ALLOCATING TIME FOR LEARNING AND GROWTH

Dedicating time to learning and personal growth is essential to personal development. This involves setting aside regular time slots for activities that contribute to learning, such as reading, taking courses, or practicing new skills. Consistency in this practice is critical to making continual progress.

Balancing structured learning with exploratory learning can enhance personal growth. Structured learning involves formal education and training, while exploratory learning includes self-directed research, experimentation, and new experiences. Both are valuable and contribute to a well-rounded personal development plan.

Overcoming the challenge of finding time for learning in a busy schedule is critical. This might involve waking up earlier, reducing time spent on less productive activities, or integrating learning into daily routines, such as listening to educational podcasts during commutes.

Learning in various formats caters to different learning styles and keeps the process engaging. This includes mixing traditional reading with audio-visual materials, hands-on experiences, and interactive learning platforms. Variety not only maintains interest but also enhances understanding and retention.

Setting specific learning goals tied to broader personal development objectives can increase the effectiveness of learning time. Whether acquiring a new skill, deepening knowledge in a particular area, or exploring a new field, having clear learning goals helps focus efforts and measure progress.

Peer learning and study groups can be an effective way to allocate time for learning. Collaborating with others provides accountability, motivation, and diverse perspectives, enriching the learning experience and making it more enjoyable.

Reflecting on what has been learned and how it applies to personal and professional life is crucial. This reflection helps integrate new knowledge and skills into one's life, ensuring that learning leads to tangible improvements and growth.

THE ROLE OF MENTORSHIP AND COACHING

Mentorship and coaching are cornerstone elements in the sphere of personal growth. A mentor or coach brings a wealth of experience and insight, offering support, guidance, and a level of accountability that can significantly hasten one's learning and development journey. They provide a unique perspective, invaluable for overcoming obstacles and making well-informed decisions.

Choosing the right mentor or coach is a crucial step. It's about finding an individual whose experiences, skills, and approach resonate with your personal growth objectives. An effective mentor or coach not only shares knowledge but also inspires and pushes you toward new heights of personal growth.

Setting clear expectations and objectives for the mentorship or coaching relationship is vital. This involves outlining your aspirations, discussing how the mentor or coach can aid in achieving these goals, and agreeing on the regularity and format of your interactions.

Active engagement and a readiness to embrace feedback are vital to fully benefiting from mentorship or coaching. This means being well-prepared for sessions, participating earnestly in discussions, and welcoming constructive criticism and advice.

Mentorship and coaching dynamics should adapt over time. As your personal development goals evolve, the focus and nature of these relationships should also shift accordingly. Continuously evaluating and recalibrating the relationship ensures its ongoing relevance and effectiveness.

Peer mentorship is another valuable resource. These are individuals on a similar journey but with differing experiences or expertise. Such relationships can be mutually enriching, providing avenues for collaborative learning and growth.

The conclusion of a formal mentorship or coaching relationship does not mark the end of its influence. The skills, knowledge, and perspectives acquired from these engagements continue to shape your personal development journey well beyond the formal period of mentorship or coaching.

LEVERAGING RESOURCES FOR SELF-IMPROVEMENT

For those dedicated to their personal growth, a treasure trove of resources is at their disposal. Utilizing these resources effectively can greatly enrich the path of self-improvement. This includes various options like books, online courses, interactive workshops, insightful podcasts, and beyond.

Choosing the right resources that resonate with your personal development objectives is crucial. Given the abundance of materials, focusing on the most pertinent and superior quality ensures that your time and effort are well spent, contributing meaningfully to your growth.

Assembling a personal development library can be a source of continuous inspiration and learning. This collection could encompass cherished books, bookmarked articles, podcasts you've saved, and notes from various courses or workshops. Having this handpicked repository readily available can be a constant wellspring of knowledge and encouragement.

Allocating time and, where needed, financial resources for these materials is important. Like budgeting for other significant areas of life, dedicating resources to personal development is an investment in yourself.

Integrating diverse types of resources can accommodate different learning styles and preferences. For instance, pairing the experiential learning of a workshop with the convenience of a podcast for reinforcement can amplify the overall learning experience.

Active engagement with these resources, as opposed to a passive approach, magnifies their effectiveness. This means jotting down notes, applying the concepts to real-life scenarios, and sharing insights with peers. Such active involvement helps in assimilating and applying the knowledge acquired.

Given the dynamic nature of personal development resources, staying abreast of the latest offerings is essential. This means watching for new publications, following industry leaders, and being receptive to exploring new areas and technologies.

OVERCOMING PLATEAUS AND STAGNATION

Personal development is not a linear journey; it often involves plateaus and periods of stagnation. Recognizing and addressing these periods is crucial for continued growth. It's about identifying when you've hit a plateau and taking proactive steps to overcome it.

One common cause of stagnation is falling into a routine that no longer challenges you. To overcome this, seek new challenges and experiences that push you out of your comfort zone. This could involve taking on a new project, learning a new skill, or changing your approach to a familiar task.

Setting new, more challenging goals can reinvigorate your personal development journey. When your current goals no longer inspire or challenge you, it's time to raise the bar. New goals can reignite your motivation and provide a fresh focus for your efforts.

Seeking feedback from others can provide insights into areas of stagnation and potential strategies for overcoming them. Sometimes, an external perspective can highlight blind spots and offer valuable suggestions for moving forward.

Taking a break or changing your environment can also help you overcome plateaus. Sometimes, stepping away from your routine and immersing yourself in a different setting can provide new perspectives and reignite your passion for growth.

Reflecting on past successes and the journey so far can provide motivation to overcome current stagnation. Remembering how far you've come and the obstacles you've already overcome can renew your confidence and determination to continue growing.

Experimenting with different methods and approaches can also help overcome plateaus. If your current strategies for personal development are no longer effective, try different techniques or approaches. Experimentation can lead to new discoveries and breakthroughs in your journey.

INTEGRATING NEW SKILLS AND KNOWLEDGE

Incorporating newly acquired skills and knowledge into your everyday life is pivotal to personal development. It goes beyond just gathering information; it's about applying it in meaningful ways that enrich your personal and professional spheres. This requires actively seeking situations where you can put new skills into practice.

Setting tangible, actionable goals for utilizing new knowledge can facilitate its practical integration. For instance, if you've learned a new communication technique, aim to apply it in your upcoming team meeting. Such purposeful application cements the learning and showcases the real-world utility of these new skills.

Sharing your newfound knowledge with others is another effective way to internalize it. Teaching others not only reinforces your own understanding but also contributes to their developmental journey.

Reflecting on the impact of these new skills and knowledge on your life and work is crucial. Such reflection evaluates the efficacy of your learning and pinpoints areas for further enhancement.

Embedding new skills into your daily routines ensures they become an intrinsic part of your life. This could mean dedicating time each day for skill practice or weaving new knowledge into your everyday tasks and responsibilities.

Soliciting feedback on your application of new skills is immensely beneficial. Input from colleagues, mentors, or coaches can offer valuable insights into your skill level and highlight areas needing additional refinement.

Understanding that integrating new skills is a continuous journey is vital. It's not a one-off event but a process that demands ongoing practice, fine-tuning, and adaptation. A commitment to continuous learning and improvement ensures the relevance and effectiveness of your skills over time.

REFLECTING AND ADJUSTING PERSONAL DEVELOPMENT PLANS

Consistent reflection is a cornerstone of personal development. It allows you to gauge your progress, celebrate your successes, and identify new growth areas. This reflective practice ensures that you remain on track with your goals and true to your values.

Adapting your personal development plan is a natural part of your growth. As you evolve, so too will your ambitions, interests, and needs. A flexible approach to revising your plan ensures it stays pertinent and impactful.

Reflection can be both structured and casual. Structured reflection might involve periodic reviews of your goals and achievements, while informal reflection could be as simple as musing over your growth during a quiet moment. Both forms are valuable and contribute to a richer understanding of your personal growth.

Incorporating feedback from others into your reflection process can offer fresh perspectives and help you view your progress through different lenses.

Documenting your personal development journey is beneficial for reflection. Maintaining a journal, portfolio, or log of your experiences and achievements provides a tangible record of your growth, serving as a source of motivation and inspiration.

Dedicating time for reflection is crucial. Amidst daily life's hustle, the need for self-reflection can often be overlooked. Setting aside regular times for reflection ensures it becomes a fundamental part of your personal development routine.

Celebrating your milestones and successes is an essential facet of reflection. Acknowledging your progress boosts morale and underscores the value of your efforts and the importance of continuing on your personal development path.

BUILDING RESILIENCE AND FLEXIBILITY

ithin the dynamic terrain of our daily lives, resilience and adaptability are crucial pillars for managing time effectively. This chapter delves into the transformative impact of fostering resilience and flexibility on our time management practices. It examines how these traits can help us steer through the unpredictability and pressures of everyday life with more grace and efficiency.

UNDERSTANDING RESILIENCE IN TIME MANAGEMENT

Resilience in time management is the capacity to recover from setbacks and adjust to new scenarios. It's about keeping your focus and staying productive, regardless of whether the disruptions are minor day-to-day issues or major life transitions. Developing resilience is essential for effective time management in various situations.

Being resilient doesn't mean strictly adhering to plans; instead, it's about adapting and progressing. It involves fostering a mindset that views challenges as avenues for growth and learning instead of as impassable barriers.

Cultivating resilience means accepting that setbacks are inherent in life and work. It's about building the inner fortitude to confront these challenges directly, rather than evading or being paralyzed by them. This strength is developed through lived experiences, reflective thinking, and a conscious effort to extend beyond your comfort zone.

A critical component of resilience is keeping a long-term view. Resilient individuals, when confronted with immediate difficulties or failures, can remember their wider objectives and values, aiding them in staying on track and keeping their drive alive.

Resilience also necessitates self-awareness and acknowledging your boundaries. It's about recognizing the right moments to persevere and when to step back and rejuvenate. Striking a balance between diligent work and proper rest is vital to sustaining resilience.

Having a supportive network can help with resilience building. Access to individuals for guidance, motivation, or just a sympathetic ear can greatly assist in navigating through challenging periods.

Exercising resilience in everyday situations strengthens this ability for more substantial challenges. Over time, this practice can revolutionize how you approach and handle time, leading to enhanced productivity and overall well-being.

ADAPTING TO CHANGING CIRCUMSTANCES

Adaptability in time management is the capacity to adjust plans and strategies in response to changing circumstances. It's about being flexible and open-minded, willing to modify approaches as new information and situations arise.

Adapting to change often requires a swift reassessment of priorities and goals. It's about quickly identifying what is most important in the new context and realigning efforts to focus on these areas.

Change can sometimes lead to unexpected opportunities. Adaptable individuals are able to recognize and seize these opportunities, turning potential disruptions into advantages. This agility can be a significant asset in both personal and professional spheres.

Adaptability also involves letting go of plans and goals that are no longer relevant or feasible. This can be challenging, but it's integral to staying aligned with current realities and making the most effective use of time.

Practicing flexibility in everyday decisions can build the skill of adaptability. This might involve trying new methods, experimenting with different approaches, or simply being open to new ideas and perspectives.

Learning from each experience of change is vital. Reflecting on what worked, what didn't, and how you adapted can provide valuable insights for future situations, enhancing your ability to manage time effectively in a dynamic environment.

Embracing change rather than resisting it is a mindset that can significantly enhance adaptability. Viewing change as an inevitable and often positive part of life can make adapting less stressful and more productive.

DEVELOPING A GROWTH MINDSET

A growth mindset, the belief that abilities and intelligence can be developed through effort and learning, is crucial in building resilience and flexibility. This mindset encourages a focus on progress and improvement rather than a fixed view of capabilities.

Cultivating a growth mindset involves embracing challenges as opportunities to learn and grow. It's about valuing the learning and development process rather than just the outcome. This perspective can transform how one approaches time management, focusing more on continual improvement and less on immediate perfection.

Fostering a growth mindset also means being open to feedback and learning from mistakes. Instead of viewing errors as failures, they are valuable learning experiences that contribute to personal and professional development.

Setting learning goals alongside performance goals can encourage a growth mindset. This might involve identifying new skills to develop, knowledge to acquire, or attitudes to cultivate, all of which contribute to a more effective approach to time management.

The language used in self-talk and communication can influence mindset. Using language that reflects learning, growth, and potential can reinforce a growth mindset in oneself and others.

Seeking new experiences and challenges is a practical way to develop a growth mindset. By stepping out of comfort zones and trying new things, individuals can expand their skills, increase their adaptability, and enhance their time management abilities.

Reflecting on personal growth over time can reinforce a growth mindset. Recognizing how much one has learned and developed can be a powerful motivator to continue seeking growth and embracing new challenges.

MANAGING STRESS AND BURNOUT

Effectively managing stress and preventing burnout are essential for maintaining resilience and flexibility. High levels of stress can hinder decision-making, reduce productivity, and impair one's ability to manage time effectively.

Identifying the sources of stress is the first step in managing it. This might involve assessing workloads, identifying challenging relationships, or recognizing personal habits that contribute to stress. Once identified, strategies can be developed to address these stressors.

Effective time management itself can be a tool for managing stress. By organizing tasks, setting priorities, and creating a balanced schedule, individuals can reduce the feeling of being overwhelmed and increase their sense of control.

Regular breaks and downtime are crucial in preventing burnout. Scheduling time for rest, relaxation, and activities that bring joy can help recharge energy and maintain a healthy perspective.

Developing coping strategies for stress, such as mindfulness practices, exercise, or hobbies, can enhance resilience. These strategies can provide an outlet for stress, improve overall well-being, and contribute to more effective time management.

Seeking support from a professional, a mentor, or a support group can be invaluable in managing stress and preventing burnout. Talking about challenges, receiving advice, or simply having someone listen to you can make a significant difference.

Balancing high-effort tasks with more enjoyable activities can also help manage stress. Allocating time for tasks that bring satisfaction or joy can provide a counterbalance to more demanding or stressful activities.

THE POWER OF POSITIVE HABITS

Developing positive habits is a crucial aspect of building resilience and flexibility. Habits, once formed, can automate positive behaviors, reducing the mental effort required to make beneficial choices and manage time effectively.

Establishing routines that support well-being and productivity can foster positive habits. This might involve morning routines that set the tone for the day, work habits that enhance efficiency, or evening routines that promote restful sleep.

Consistency is crucial in habit formation. Regularly practicing a behavior makes it more likely to become a habit. Setting specific times for these behaviors helps maintain consistency.

Positive habits should be aligned with personal goals and values. Habits that are meaningful and contribute to one's broader objectives are more likely to be maintained and positively impact time management.

Small, incremental changes are often more effective in building lasting habits. Starting with small steps and gradually building on them can make the process of habit formation less daunting and more sustainable.

Celebrating small victories in habit formation can provide motivation and reinforcement. Recognizing progress, even in small increments, can encourage continued effort and commitment to developing positive habits.

Reflecting on the impact of habits on time management and overall well-being is essential. Regularly assessing how habits are contributing to (or detracting from) your goals can help you make necessary adjustments and ensure that your habits serve you effectively.

EMBRACING UNCERTAINTY AND RISK

Embracing uncertainty and risk is an integral part of building resilience and flexibility. In a constantly changing world, navigating uncertainty and taking calculated risks can enhance one's ability to manage time effectively and seize opportunities.

Developing a tolerance for uncertainty involves accepting that not everything can be planned or controlled. It's about being comfortable with ambiguity and making decisions even when not all information is available.

Taking calculated risks can lead to significant rewards, both in personal growth and in achieving goals. This involves assessing potential risks and benefits, making informed decisions, and being prepared to learn from the outcome, whatever it may be.

Flexibility and adaptability are key to embracing uncertainty. Adjusting plans, changing direction, or pivoting strategies in response to new information or changing circumstances is crucial for effective time management in an uncertain environment.

Building a support network can provide a safety net when navigating uncertainty and risk. Having people to turn to for advice, encouragement, or perspective can make stepping into the unknown less daunting.

Learning from experiences, both successes and failures, is a vital part of embracing uncertainty. Each experience provides valuable lessons that can inform future decisions and approaches, enhancing one's ability to manage time and life's uncertainties.

Practicing decision-making in uncertain situations can strengthen this ability. Making small decisions in the face of uncertainty and reflecting on the outcomes can build confidence and skills for navigating more significant uncertainties and risks.

CULTIVATING EMOTIONAL INTELLIGENCE

Emotional Intelligence (EI) is the skill of comprehending and managing one's emotions and empathizing with others. In time management, EI is instrumental in fostering resilience, effectively handling stress, and engaging productively with others.

At the heart of EI lies self-awareness. This entails an in-depth understanding of your emotions, strengths, weak-nesses, and triggers. Such awareness can influence how you organize your time, react to stress, and engage with others.

Another facet of EI is self-regulation, which is the ability to control your emotional responses, especially in high-pres-sure or challenging situations. Proficient self-regulation helps avoid hasty decisions or actions that could derail your time management strategies.

Empathy, or the capacity to comprehend and resonate with others' feelings, can significantly bolster relationships and teamwork. Within a group, empathy fosters more trans-parent communication, stronger bonds, and a supportive atmosphere, all contributing to enhanced time management and productivity.

Developing social skills, a crucial aspect of EI, is vital for effec-tively navigating interpersonal relationships. This includes honing clear communication, resolving conflicts construc-tively, and cultivating robust, cooperative relationships. Strong social skills can save time by preventing misunder-standings and promoting a collaborative work environment.

Practicing mindfulness and engaging in self-reflection are powerful ways to boost EI. Mindfulness aids in maintaining present-moment awareness, while self-reflection offers insights into emotional patterns and behaviors. Both prac-tices are key to better self-management and more empathetic interactions with others.

Feedback from others is a valuable resource in developing EI. It provides an external viewpoint on your emotional expression and behavior and can highlight areas for improvement. Actively seeking and positively responding to feedback is essential in enhancing EI.

Emotional intelligence is also pivotal in managing stress and preventing burnout. By effectively navigating one's emotional landscape, it's possible to maintain a composed and clear perspective, even in challenging scenarios, leading to more efficient time management and decision-making.

EFFECTIVE COMMUNICATION
AND TIME MANAGEMENT

*I*n *today's world, where work and personal life are intricately linked, the quality of our communication significantly influences our time management. Skillful communication can conserve time, avert misunderstandings, and boost productivity, whereas ineffective communication can result in delays and irritation. This chapter delves into honing communication skills that optimize time, streamline teamwork, establish explicit boundaries, utilize technology for better communication, manage excess communication, promote brevity and clarity, and effectively give and receive feedback.*

MASTERING TIME-SAVING COMMUNICATION SKILLS

Effective communication skills are indispensable for saving time. Mastering these skills involves being clear, concise, and purposeful in your interactions. It's about getting your message across efficiently without unnecessary repetition or ambiguity.

Active listening is a crucial aspect of time-saving communication. By fully focusing on the speaker, understanding their message, and responding appropriately, you can avoid misunderstandings and the need for repetitive follow-up communications.

Choosing the right communication medium is essential. Some messages are best conveyed in person or over the phone, while others can be effectively communicated via email or messaging apps. Selecting the appropriate medium can save time and ensure your message is received and understood as intended.

Time-saving communication also involves being prepared. Whether it's a meeting, a presentation, or a casual conversation, coming prepared with critical points and objectives can make the interaction more efficient and productive.

Regularly reviewing and refining your communication habits is important. Reflect on your interactions and consider how you might communicate more effectively in the future. Continuous improvement in communication skills can lead to significant time savings over time.

Developing a personal communication style that is effective yet authentic can enhance the efficiency of your interactions. A style that reflects your personality and respects others' preferences fosters smoother and quicker exchanges.

Using clarifying and summarizing techniques in conversations can ensure that all parties are on the same page, which is essential for preventing miscommunications and the time wasted in resolving them.

MANAGING TIME IN MEETINGS AND COLLABORATIONS

Meetings and collaborative projects are common in most work environments, but they can be significant time sinks if not managed properly. Effective time management in these settings is crucial for maintaining productivity and meeting goals.

Planning meetings with a clear purpose and agenda can significantly improve their effectiveness. Ensure that every meeting has specific objectives that are communicated to all participants in advance.

Keeping meetings focused and on track is essential. Stick to the agenda and gently steer discussions back on course if they begin to drift. Time limits for each agenda item help maintain focus and prevent overruns.

Only invite the necessary participants to meetings. Having too many people in a meeting can slow decision-making and lead to longer, less productive sessions.

For collaborative projects, clear communication of roles, responsibilities, and deadlines is key. This clarity helps ensure that everyone knows what is expected of them and can manage their time accordingly.

Using collaborative tools and platforms can streamline communication and coordination in team projects. These tools can provide a centralized space for sharing information, tracking progress, and facilitating discussions, saving time and reducing the need for frequent meetings.

Regular check-ins and updates are important in collaborative efforts. They keep everyone aligned and informed, reducing the need for additional meetings or lengthy email threads.

Encouraging a culture of punctuality and respect for others' time in meetings and collaborations is essential. Starting and ending meetings on time and sticking to the agreed-upon schedule shows respect for participants' time and sets a standard for efficient time use.

SETTING EXPECTATIONS AND BOUNDARIES

Clear communication of expectations and boundaries is crucial for effective time management. It helps prevent misunderstandings, sets the stage for productive interactions, and respects everyone's time.

Setting expectations involves being clear about what is required, when it is needed, and what the standards are. Clear expectations can prevent wasted time and effort, whether it's with colleagues, clients, or family members.

Communicating boundaries is about letting others know your availability and how you prefer to be communicated with. This might involve specifying preferred meeting times, setting email response times, or establishing 'quiet hours' for focused work.

Negotiating expectations and boundaries is sometimes necessary, especially in collaborative or team settings. Being open to discussion and compromise can lead to a mutually agreeable arrangement that respects everyone's time and needs.

Regularly revisiting and communicating any changes in your expectations and boundaries is important. As your circumstances and responsibilities change, so too might your needs and limitations.

Being assertive yet respectful when setting expectations and boundaries is critical. It's about valuing your own time and needs while being considerate of others.

Modeling the behavior you expect from others regarding respecting time and boundaries can be very effective. Leading by example can encourage a culture of mutual respect and efficiency.

LEVERAGING TECHNOLOGY FOR EFFECTIVE COMMUNICATION

Technology offers many tools and platforms to enhance communication, but using them effectively is key to saving time. Leveraging technology wisely can streamline communication processes, reduce misunderstandings, and enhance collaboration.

Choosing the right communication tools is essential. Whether it's email, instant messaging, video conferencing, or project management software, selecting tools that meet your specific needs and those of your team can make communication more efficient.

Using technology to automate routine communications can save a significant amount of time. Automated reminders, scheduled emails, and template responses can streamline repetitive tasks and free up time for more complex interactions.

Balancing the use of technology with personal interaction is important. While technology can enhance communication, it cannot replace the nuances and depth of face-to-face inter-actions. Knowing when to switch from digital communica-tion to personal interaction can improve understanding and relationship building.

Managing your digital communication tools to prevent them from becoming distractions is crucial. This might involve setting specific times to check emails, turning off unneces-sary notifications, or using 'do not disturb' features during focused work periods.

Using technology to facilitate asynchronous communication can be particularly effective in managing time differences and busy schedules. Tools that allow for communication that doesn't require immediate responses can reduce the pressure on all parties and allow for more thoughtful, well-considered interactions.

Regularly evaluating and updating the technology tools you use for communication can ensure they remain effective. As technology evolves and your needs change, reassessing and adapting your tools can improve communication efficiency.

DEALING WITH COMMUNICATION OVERLOAD

In today's fast-paced world, communication overload is a common challenge. Managing this overload effectively is vital to maintaining focus and productivity.

Recognizing the signs of communication overload is the first step in addressing it. This might involve feeling over-whelmed by the volume of emails, struggling to keep up with messages, or feeling constantly distracted by communication demands.

Prioritizing communications can help manage overload. Not all messages require immediate attention. Learning to quickly assess the importance and urgency of communications and prioritize them accordingly can prevent overwhelm.

Setting aside specific times for dealing with communications can be effective. This might involve dedicating certain times of the day for email, calls, or meetings, allowing for focused work periods free from communication distractions.

Using filters and folders to organize digital communications can also help manage overload. Sorting messages into categories and setting up rules for handling different types of communications can streamline the process and reduce the time spent on email management.

Learning to say no to unnecessary communication is essential. Whether it's declining meeting invitations that aren't relevant or unsubscribing from unneeded email lists, reducing the volume of incoming communications can alleviate overload.

Taking breaks from digital communication can provide much-needed relief. Regular digital detoxes, even if only for a short period, can help reset your focus and reduce the stress of constant connectivity.

CULTIVATING CONCISENESS AND CLARITY

Conciseness and clarity in communication are essential for effective time management. They help convey your message more efficiently, reducing the need for follow-up explanations and clarifications.

Practicing conciseness involves being direct and to the point in your communications. It's about conveying your message in as few words as necessary without sacrificing clarity. This not only saves time for you but also for the recipient.

Clarity is about making your communication easily understandable. This involves using straightforward language, avoiding jargon or ambiguous terms, and being specific in your requests or information.

Preparing in advance can help make the information concise and clear. Whether it's a meeting, a presentation, or an email, thinking through what you want to say beforehand can help you communicate more effectively.

Asking for feedback on your communication style can provide insights into how clear and concise you are. Feedback from others can help you identify areas for improvement and enhance your communication skills.

Practicing active listening can also contribute to conciseness and clarity. You can respond more effectively by fully understanding what others are saying, reducing the need for prolonged exchanges.

Being aware of your audience and tailoring your communication to their needs and understanding can enhance clarity. Different audiences may require different levels of detail or explanations, so adjusting your communication accordingly can improve understanding and efficiency.

FEEDBACK: GIVING AND RECEIVING

Feedback is a critical component of effective communication and time management. Giving and receiving feedback helps improve performance, clarify expectations, and foster personal and professional growth.

Giving constructive feedback involves being specific, focusing on behaviors rather than personal attributes, and offering suggestions for improvement. It's about providing helpful and actionable feedback, enabling the recipient to make positive changes.

Receiving feedback with an open mind is equally important. It involves listening without becoming defensive, considering the feedback objectively, and using it as an opportunity for growth. When received constructively, even negative feedback can be a valuable learning experience.

Creating a culture where feedback is regularly given and received can enhance team communication and time management. Regular feedback can prevent misunderstandings, clarify expectations, and foster a more open, collaborative environment.

Timing and delivery are crucial in giving feedback. Choose an appropriate time and setting for feedback, and deliver it in a respectful and considerate manner. The way feedback is given can significantly impact how it is received and acted upon.

Encouraging a two-way feedback process can lead to more effective communication. Allowing for feedback from the recipient can provide insights into their perspective and help you understand the impact of your communication style. It creates a dialogue that can lead to mutual understanding and improvement.

Balancing positive feedback with constructive criticism is essential. Recognizing and acknowledging what someone is doing well, along with areas for improvement, can make feedback more palatable and motivating. It shows that you value the individual's efforts and are invested in their growth.

Regular self-reflection on how you give and receive feedback can enhance your effectiveness. Reflect on your feedback interactions and consider how you might improve. Are you clear and specific? Do you listen openly to feedback? Self-reflection helps refine your approach to feedback over time.

Seeking feedback proactively demonstrates a commitment to improvement and effective communication. Don't wait for feedback to be offered; ask for it. This proactive approach can lead to personal and professional growth and development.

Using feedback to set goals and action plans can transform it into a powerful tool for development. Instead of just receiving feedback passively, use it to set specific, actionable goals for improvement. This approach turns feedback into a catalyst for positive change.

LEVERAGING TIME FOR HEALTH
AND WELLNESS

*I*n an era of ever-increasing speed and demands, dedicating time to health and wellness is essential, transcending mere luxury. This chapter explores the essential equilibrium of sustaining health within the confines of hectic schedules. It integrates crucial aspects like exercise, nutrition, mindfulness, adequate sleep, stress management, and comprehensive wellness practices into practical time management approaches. Each of these components is fundamental to boosting overall well-being, which, in turn, enhances productivity and efficiency.

BALANCING HEALTH WITH BUSY SCHEDULES

Juggling health and wellness with demanding schedules is a common challenge. The key lies in recognizing health as a priority, not an afterthought. Integrating health practices into daily routines ensures they are not overlooked in the hustle of daily commitments.

Effective time management for health begins with planning. Scheduling time for exercise, meal preparation, and relaxation just as one would for work tasks can ensure these activities are given the attention they deserve. Viewing these activities as non-negotiable appointments with oneself can reinforce their importance.

Flexibility is crucial in balancing health with busy schedules. This might involve adjusting exercise routines to fit a changing schedule or preparing healthy meals in advance for busy days. Being adaptable in approach allows for maintaining health practices even during the busiest times.

Incorporating health and wellness activities into everyday life can be an effective strategy. For example, opting for walking or cycling to work, using standing desks, or choosing stairs over elevators are ways to integrate physical activity into daily routines.

Identifying and eliminating time wasters can free up time for health activities. This involves assessing one's schedule for unproductive activities or inefficiencies and reallocating that time to health-promoting activities.

Seeking support and accountability can help in maintaining health routines. Whether partnering with a friend for workouts or joining a health-focused group, having others to share the journey with can provide motivation and encouragement.

Health and wellness should be tailored to individual needs and preferences. What works for one person may not work for another. Understanding and respecting one's body and needs is crucial for creating a sustainable and effective health and wellness routine.

EXERCISE AND TIME MANAGEMENT

Exercise is a vital component of a healthy lifestyle, and managing time to incorporate regular physical activity is essential. Regular exercise improves physical health and enhances mental well-being, leading to increased productivity and better time management.

Finding the right time of day for exercise can enhance its benefits. Some people prefer morning workouts to energize their day, while others may find evening exercises an excellent way to unwind. Experimenting with different times can help identify when exercise feels best and is most sustainable.

Consistency is more important than duration in exercise routines. Short, regular exercise sessions can be more effective and manageable than infrequent, longer workouts. Even 10-15 minutes of physical activity can have significant health benefits.

Incorporating a variety of physical activities can prevent boredom and improve overall fitness. This might include a mix of cardiovascular exercises, strength training, flexibility exercises, and balance activities. Variety not only keeps exercise interesting but also ensures a well-rounded approach to fitness.

Setting realistic and achievable fitness goals can provide direction and motivation. Whether it's improving endurance, strength, flexibility, or simply staying active, having clear goals can help focus your efforts and make exercise a valued part of your routine.

Integrating exercise into other daily activities can be an effective way to manage time. This could involve exercises at your desk, walking meetings, or family activities that include physical movement. Making exercise a part of your daily life can help ensure other commitments don't sideline it.

Listening to your body and adjusting exercise routines as needed is important. Respecting your body's signals, whether it's needing rest or being ready for more challenge, ensures that exercise remains beneficial and doesn't lead to burnout or injury.

NUTRITION AND TIME

Nutrition is a crucial pillar in maintaining health and wellness, making managing time effectively to accommodate healthy eating habits vital. Adequate nutrition fuels the body for daily tasks and underpins long-term health.

Pre-planning meals can significantly streamline your routine and alleviate stress. This could involve allocating a specific time each week for meal planning, shopping for ingredients, and some meal prep. A structured plan helps to circumvent impromptu and often less healthy eating choices.

Fitting healthy eating into a hectic schedule may seem daunting, but it is entirely achievable with specific strategies. This can include keeping healthy snacks within easy reach, opting for quick yet nutritious meal choices, and avoiding the habit of skipping meals.

Bulk cooking and smart use of leftovers offer efficient methods to maintain a healthy diet. Cooking larger batches for use over several days minimizes cooking time and ensures you always have healthy options readily available.

Mindful eating is also pivotal in managing nutrition effectively. This means tuning into your body's hunger signals, eating without distractions, and savoring your meals, leading to more enjoyable and healthy eating experiences.

Hydration, simple yet crucial, is often overlooked in nutrition. Carrying a water bottle and setting reminders to drink water can help maintain hydration, which is vital for overall health and energy levels.

Finally, striking a balance between nutritional needs and enjoying food is essential. While it's important to prioritize healthy eating, allowing for occasional treats and relishing a variety of foods can make adhering to a nutritious diet both sustainable and pleasurable.

MINDFULNESS AND MEDITATION

Integrating mindfulness and meditation into your daily regimen can profoundly impact your mental health and your approach to time management. These practices diminish stress, sharpen focus, and foster a more composed and mindful approach to everyday activities.

Mindfulness is the art of inhabiting the present moment and engaging wholeheartedly with the task at hand. This practice can transform even the most ordinary tasks into more enriching experiences, enhancing both focus and productivity.

Even brief sessions of meditation can yield significant benefits for mental clarity and function. Consistent practice can alleviate stress, sharpen concentration, and bolster decision-making abilities, all of which are conducive to more efficient time management.

Mindfulness can be woven into daily activities with ease. Techniques include engaging in mindful breathing during breaks, fully concentrating on the current task, or practicing gratitude throughout your day.

Carving out specific times for meditation can foster a regular practice. Whether it's a moment of quiet in the morning, an evening wind-down, or a short break during your workday, a set schedule for meditation can help integrate it into your daily life.

Mindfulness and meditation apps can offer direction and structure for those new to these practices. With various practices at your fingertips, these tools are convenient for incorporating mindfulness and meditation into a hectic schedule.

Reflecting on how mindfulness and meditation enhance your daily life can solidify your commitment to the practice. Observing changes in your stress levels, attentiveness, or general well-being can encourage the ongoing practice and deeper exploration of these techniques.

Remember, mindfulness and meditation are highly personal practices. Exploring various methods to discover what resonates with you is essential for effectively incorporating these practices into your time management and overall wellness strategy.

SLEEP AND PRODUCTIVITY

The relationship between sleep and productivity is often underestimated. Quality sleep is crucial for cognitive function, mood regulation, and overall health, directly impacting time management and productivity.

Prioritizing sleep in your schedule is essential. This involves setting consistent sleep and wake times, creating a bedtime routine that signals to your body that it's time to wind down, and ensuring you get the recommended amount of sleep each night.

Creating an environment conducive to good sleep can enhance its quality. This might include a comfortable mattress and pillows, a cool and dark room, and minimizing noise and distractions. A sleep-friendly environment can lead to more restful and rejuvenating sleep.

Managing time to include relaxation and winding-down activities before bed can improve sleep quality. Activities such as reading, gentle stretching, or listening to calming music can help prepare the mind and body for rest.

Understanding and respecting your body's natural sleep-wake cycle, or circadian rhythm, can improve sleep and energy levels. Aligning your schedule with your natural rhythm as much as possible can lead to better sleep and more productive waking hours.

Limiting exposure to screens before bedtime is essential. Screens' blue light can obstruct the body's ability to produce melatonin, which controls sleep. Reducing screen time in the evening can help ensure better sleep quality.

Napping can be a useful tool for managing energy levels, but it should be done strategically. Short naps of around 20 minutes can be refreshing without interfering with night-time sleep. Timing naps earlier in the afternoon can prevent them from disrupting your sleep schedule.

STRESS MANAGEMENT TECHNIQUES

Managing stress effectively is essential for sustaining health, well-being, and efficiency. Prolonged stress not only leads to various health complications but can also significantly disrupt efficient time management.

The initial step in stress management is identifying what specifically triggers your stress. Once these triggers are recognized, you can devise methods to avoid or handle them more effectively.

Engaging in physical activities is an excellent way to alleviate stress. Consistent exercise reduces stress hormones, enhances mood, and promotes overall health. Integrating enjoyable physical activities into your routine can be a practical approach to stress management.

Employing relaxation techniques like deep breathing, progressive muscle relaxation, or yoga can effectively diminish stress. These practices aid in soothing both the mind and body, lowering stress levels, and fostering heightened focus and productivity.

Establishing realistic goals and expectations is another way to mitigate stress. Overextending oneself or setting unattainable objectives can lead to frustration and increased stress. Setting feasible goals aligned with your capabilities can help maintain manageable stress levels.

Reaching out for social support is a valuable tool for managing stress. Discussing your stressors with friends, family, or coworkers can offer comfort and may provide fresh insights and coping strategies.

Regular breaks throughout your day can also significantly affect stress management. Taking short pauses for relaxation or engaging in different activities can refresh your focus and lower stress.

HOLISTIC WELLNESS APPROACHES

Embracing a holistic view of wellness means acknowledging the interconnectedness of physical, mental, emotional, and social well-being and their collective impact on time management. This comprehensive mindset recognizes that each wellness dimension affects the others, contributing to more balanced and efficient time management.

Integrating diverse wellness practices into everyday life can boost overall well-being. This could include a blend of physical exercise, nutritious eating, mental health activities, and engaging in social endeavors. A holistic approach ensures a well-rounded routine that caters to every facet of health.

It's vital to understand the link between physical and mental health. Physical activities enhance physical fitness and bolster mental and emotional health, leading to improved concentration and productivity.

Social wellness, defined by the quality of your relationships and social interactions, significantly influences your overall health and efficiency in managing time. Cultivating positive relationships and a supportive network offers emotional backing, helps alleviate stress, and increases overall life satisfaction.

Managing emotional well-being involves effectively understanding and handling your emotions. Techniques like journaling, therapy, or mindfulness can aid in recognizing and controlling emotions, subsequently improving decision-making and time management.

Spiritual wellness provides a sense of purpose and perspective, whether through religious practices, meditation, or a connection with nature. This aspect of wellness can assist in aligning your time management with your deeper values and objectives.

Maintaining a balance between work and leisure activities is an essential element of a holistic approach to wellness. Allocating time for hobbies, relaxation, and personal interests is crucial to achieving a healthy work-life balance.

Regularly reviewing and adapting your wellness practices ensures they stay practical and pertinent. As your needs and life circumstances evolve, so should your wellness strategies. Continual evaluation and adjustment of your practices can lead to sustained health and time management improvements.

STRATEGIC PLANNING AND GOAL SETTING

*S*trategic planning and goal-setting stand as key pillars in the architecture of proficient time management. This involves visualizing a preferred future, defining achievable objectives, and developing a detailed plan to realize those goals. This chapter talks about how to make good long-term plans, setting SMART (Specific, Measurable, Achievable, Relevant, Time-bound) goals, understanding the important role of vision in planning, breaking goals down into smaller steps, being ready for the unexpected, making sure that goals are in line with personal values, and the important habit of going back to these plans often and making them better.

CRAFTING EFFECTIVE LONG-TERM PLANS

Effective long-term planning is anchored in a lucid vision of your desired future. It involves crafting a vivid, detailed picture of where you aspire to be. Such plans act as compasses, offering direction and purpose and aiding in making choices that resonate with your ultimate goals.

The process of long-term planning strikes a balance between ambition and practicality. It's about creating aspirational and attainable goals, stretching your abilities while remaining feasible given your existing resources and limitations.

Incorporating adaptability into your long-term plans is crucial, given life's inherent unpredictability. Being flexible allows you to modify your plans in response to unexpected changes while still keeping your ultimate objectives in sight.

Comprehensive long-term planning should encompass various facets of life, including career, education, personal development, and other key areas. A holistic approach ensures that all significant aspects are addressed, leading to a well-rounded and balanced plan.

Establishing clear benchmarks within your long-term plans is instrumental for monitoring progress. These milestones function as progress indicators, helping you evaluate your journey and understand the tasks that lie ahead.

Seeking input from mentors, advisors, or peers during the planning phase can offer invaluable perspectives. Their insights can reveal potential challenges and provide alternative strategies that might not have occurred to you.

Periodically revisiting and updating your long-term plans is vital. As you evolve and your circumstances change, your plans should also transform. Regular reviews help keep your plans pertinent and in sync with your changing goals and life situation.

SETTING AND ACHIEVING SMART GOALS

SMART goals—specific, measurable, achievable, relevant, and time-bound—are essential to effective goal-setting. They provide a clear framework that makes goals tangible and actionable, increasing the likelihood of achievement.

Specificity in goal-setting helps in focusing efforts. Clearly defined goals leave no room for ambiguity, making planning and taking action easier. They answer the what, why, and how of your objectives.

Measurability allows for tracking progress. When goals are measurable, it's possible to see how much has been accomplished and how far you are from your target, which can be highly motivating.

Achievability ensures that goals are realistic. While it's important to aim high, setting goals that are within reach and considering your resources and constraints prevents frustration and keeps you motivated.

Relevance is about ensuring that your goals align with your larger plans and values. Goals that are meaningful and relevant to you are more likely to be pursued with passion and commitment.

Time-bound goals have a sense of urgency. They have clear deadlines, which help prioritize tasks, maintain momentum, and prevent procrastination.

Breaking down large goals into smaller, more manageable tasks makes them less daunting. It also provides opportunities for small victories along the way, boosting confidence and motivation.

Regularly reviewing and adjusting your goals is important. As you make progress, face challenges, or experience changes in your circumstances, your goals may need to be revised to remain relevant and achievable.

THE ROLE OF VISION IN PLANNING

Vision is the foundation of effective strategic planning. It's the big picture of what you want to achieve—a clear and compelling image of the desired future that guides your planning and goal-setting.

A strong vision provides direction and purpose. It serves as a north star, helping you stay focused on your long-term objectives, even when faced with challenges and distractions.

Developing a vision involves deep introspection and imagination. It's about considering your ideal future—personal, professional, and beyond. A well-crafted vision is inspiring and motivating.

Communicating your vision to others, whether team members, family, or friends, can garner support and create a shared understanding. It helps in aligning efforts and fosters collaboration towards common goals.

The vision should be ambitious yet attainable. While it should stretch your capabilities, it should also be grounded in reality, considering your current situation and potential.

Incorporating flexibility into your vision is important. As you grow and evolve, so too will your vision. Being open to modifying your vision ensures that it remains relevant and inspiring.

Reflecting on your vision regularly can reinforce your commitment to your goals and plans. It serves as a reminder of what you're working towards and why, keeping you motivated and focused.

BREAKING DOWN GOALS INTO MANAGEABLE STEPS

Breaking down large goals into smaller, manageable steps is critical to effective planning. It makes goals less overwhelming and provides a clear path to achievement.

Each step should be actionable and concrete. Rather than vague tasks, steps should be specific actions that move you closer to your goal. This clarity makes it easier to take action and track progress.

Assigning timelines and deadlines to each step helps maintain momentum and prevents procrastination. It creates a sense of urgency and helps you prioritize tasks related to your goals.

Celebrating the completion of each step can boost motivation. Acknowledging these small victories reinforces positive behavior and motivates you towards the larger goal.

Regularly reviewing your progress at each step allows for adjustments as needed. If a particular approach isn't working or circumstances have changed, you can modify your steps to stay on track.

Balancing the focus on immediate steps with an eye on the larger goal is important. While it's necessary to concentrate on the task at hand, keeping the larger goal in mind ensures that each step is aligned with your ultimate objective.

Seeking feedback on your progress at each step can provide valuable insights. Feedback from mentors, peers, or coaches can help you assess your approach and make the necessary adjustments.

PLANNING FOR CONTINGENCIES

Contingency planning is an essential part of strategic planning and goal-setting. It involves anticipating potential obstacles or changes and developing plans to address them. This proactive approach ensures that you're prepared for various scenarios and can continue progressing toward your goals.

Identifying potential risks and obstacles early in the planning process is vital. This involves considering what could go wrong and its impact on your goals. Being aware of potential challenges helps in developing effective contingency plans.

Developing alternative plans or backup options for each identified risk ensures you're not caught off guard. These plans provide a course of action if the original plan becomes unfeasible, allowing you to continue moving toward your goal.

Regularly assessing the likelihood and impact of potential risks helps prioritize contingency planning efforts. Focus on developing plans for the most likely or impactful risks to ensure efficient use of time and resources.

Flexibility is crucial in contingency planning. Adapting quickly to changing circumstances or unexpected challenges is key to maintaining progress toward your goals.

Testing and revising contingency plans is important. As situations evolve, previously developed plans may no longer be relevant or effective. Regularly reviewing and updating these plans ensures they remain useful.

Incorporating lessons learned from past challenges into contingency planning can enhance its effectiveness. Reflecting on how previous obstacles were handled and what could have been done differently provides valuable insights for future planning.

ALIGNING GOALS WITH PERSONAL VALUES

Aligning goals with personal values is essential for meaningful and sustainable success. Goals that align with your values are more likely to be pursued with passion and commitment, leading to greater fulfillment and satisfaction.

Understanding your core values is the first step in aligning your goals with them. This involves introspection and possibly a reevaluation of what truly matters to you. Clear values provide a framework for setting goals that are meaningful and fulfilling.

Setting goals that reflect your values enhances motivation. When goals are aligned with what you deeply care about, they become more than just tasks to be completed; they become part of your life's purpose.

Balancing goal achievement with value alignment can sometimes be challenging. It may involve making difficult decisions or trade-offs. However, in the long run, goals that are aligned with your values lead to more sustainable and satisfying achievements.

Regularly reviewing your goals and their alignment with your values is important. As you grow and evolve, so too will your values and priorities. Ensuring that your goals continue to reflect your values is key to maintaining motivation and fulfillment.

Incorporating values into your daily routines and habits reinforces their importance. By living your values in your everyday actions, you reinforce their significance and ensure that your goals remain aligned with them.

Seeking feedback from trusted individuals can provide insights into how well your goals align with your values. These perspectives can help you assess your goals and make adjustments to ensure they align with your core values.

REGULAR REVIEW AND ADJUSTMENT OF PLANS

Regularly reviewing and updating plans is a vital aspect of successful strategic planning. These revisions ensure that your plans and objectives stay relevant, attainable, and aligned with your evolving circumstances and priorities.

Setting aside time for periodic reviews of your plans is crucial to maintaining clarity and direction. Whether these reviews occur weekly, monthly, or quarterly, they offer a chance to gauge progress, pinpoint challenges, and implement necessary modifications.

In these review sessions, it's important to evaluate not just the outcomes but also the processes. Reflect on the strategies and tactics employed and assess their continued efficacy or the need for alternative approaches.

Flexibility in adjusting plans is critical. Adapting your plans as new information emerges or situations evolve ensures they stay effective and pertinent. Adaptability in your planning process is crucial for staying aligned with changing realities.

Incorporating feedback during review sessions can significantly improve the quality of your plans. Insights from mentors, peers, or coaches can offer fresh perspectives and ideas for refinement and enhancement.

Documenting any changes and adjustments to your plans is a valuable historical record. This documentation can be a helpful resource for future planning endeavors and offers insights into your growth and decision-making processes.

Recognizing and celebrating progress during these reviews is also important. Acknowledging even the most minor achievements can be a substantial morale booster. It's about valuing the effort and progress made, which can be a powerful motivator to persist in pursuing your broader goals.

OPTIMIZING WORK ENVIRONMENTS

*I*n today's dynamic professional world, fine-tuning work environments is key to mastering time management. This chapter delves into various strategies for cultivating efficient workspaces. It covers optimizing physical and digital spaces for productivity, harnessing technology to its full potential, effectively managing time in remote and hybrid work scenarios, nurturing supportive team environments, navigating the intricacies of office politics, achieving a harmonious balance between professional and personal life, and adapting to the continuously evolving trends in the workplace. These components are essential in boosting productivity, preserving a healthy work-life balance, and remaining adaptable amid the ever-changing work landscape.

CREATING PRODUCTIVE WORKSPACES

The design and organization of a workspace can significantly impact productivity and time management. A well-organized, clutter-free environment minimizes distractions and aids focus, making time spent at work more effective.

Personalizing your workspace to suit your needs and preferences can enhance comfort and efficiency. Whether it's ergonomic furniture, the proper lighting, or personal items that inspire or relax, creating a space where you feel at ease can improve your work experience.

Minimizing distractions is a key aspect of a productive workspace. This might involve noise-canceling headphones in a busy office, setting boundaries in a home office, or using tools to block digital distractions.

Regularly reevaluating and adjusting your workspace is essential. As your tasks and responsibilities evolve, so too might your workspace needs. Periodic assessments ensure that your environment continues to support your productivity.

Adequate storage and organization systems can significantly improve workspace efficiency. Having a place for everything and keeping things in their place reduces the time spent searching for items and helps maintain focus.

Incorporating elements that promote well-being, such as plants, artwork, or access to natural light, can enhance the overall quality of your work environment, leading to better focus and reduced stress.

Experimenting with different layouts or arrangements can help identify the most productive setup for your workspace. Sometimes, small changes can have a significant impact on comfort and productivity.

LEVERAGING TECHNOLOGY WISELY

When used wisely, technology can be a powerful tool for enhancing time management. However, it's important to use technology to support, rather than hinder, productivity.

Selecting the right tools is crucial. Whether it's project management software, communication platforms, or productivity apps, choosing tools that align with your work style and needs can make a significant difference.

Setting boundaries with technology can prevent it from becoming a distraction. This might involve designated times to check emails, turning off non-essential notifications, or using software that limits time on certain websites or apps.

Using technology to automate routine tasks can save time for more complex or creative work. Automation tools can handle tasks like scheduling, data entry, or even certain aspects of customer service.

Staying updated on new technologies and tools can provide a competitive edge and increase efficiency. Regularly exploring and experimenting with new tools can uncover better ways to manage tasks and time.

Balancing the use of technology with the need for human interaction is important. While technology can streamline many processes, it cannot replace the nuances and benefits of face-to-face communication and collaboration.

Regularly evaluating the effectiveness of your technology tools and practices ensures they continue to meet your needs. As your responsibilities and tasks evolve, so too might the technology solutions that best support them.

TIME MANAGEMENT IN REMOTE AND HYBRID WORK

Remote and hybrid work environments present unique time management challenges and opportunities. The flexibility they offer can enhance productivity but also requires self-discipline and effective time management skills.

Establishing a routine in remote work is key to maintaining structure and productivity. Regular start and end times, designated break periods, and consistent daily rituals can provide a sense of normalcy and discipline.

Creating a dedicated workspace in a remote setting helps mentally separate work from personal life. A specific area for work, even if it's a small space, can help you focus and signal to others that you are in work mode.

Managing distractions in a home environment is crucial. This involves setting boundaries with family or housemates, managing personal tasks so they don't infringe on work time, and creating an environment conducive to focus.

Staying connected with colleagues and supervisors in remote settings is important for collaboration and maintaining a sense of team. Regular check-ins, virtual meetings, and collaborative tools can help bridge the physical distance.

Balancing flexibility with accountability is a crucial aspect of remote work. While remote work allows for schedule flexibility, maintaining accountability for tasks and responsibilities ensures that work remains on track.

Adapting to hybrid work environments involves navigating the best of both worlds—office and remote work. This might involve designating specific tasks or activities for each setting based on where they can be most effectively completed.

BUILDING A SUPPORTIVE TEAM CULTURE

A supportive team culture is vital for effective time management and overall productivity. It fosters collaboration, mutual respect, and a shared commitment to goals, which can significantly enhance team efficiency.

Encouraging open communication and collaboration within teams helps streamline tasks and avoid misunderstandings. Creating an environment where team members feel comfortable sharing ideas, asking for help, and offering support is key.

Recognizing and valuing each team member's contributions can strengthen the team dynamic. Acknowledging individual efforts and skills encourages a culture of respect and appreciation, which can improve morale and productivity.

Fostering a sense of collective responsibility and accountability enhances team effectiveness. When team members feel accountable for their own tasks and the team's overall success, it promotes a more collaborative and efficient work environment.

Providing opportunities for team development and growth can enhance team dynamics. Whether through team-building activities, training sessions, or collaborative projects, investing in team development can yield significant benefits in terms of productivity and cohesion.

Resolving conflicts promptly and constructively is important for maintaining a supportive team culture. Addressing issues as they arise prevents them from escalating and impacting team dynamics and productivity.

Celebrating team achievements and milestones can boost morale and reinforce a positive team culture. Recognizing collective successes strengthens the sense of team unity and shared purpose.

NAVIGATING OFFICE POLITICS AND TIME WASTERS

Office politics and time-wasting activities can be significant barriers to productivity. Navigating these challenges effectively is important for maintaining focus and managing time efficiently.

Identifying and avoiding unnecessary political battles is crucial. Engaging in office politics can be draining and distracting. Focusing on your work and maintaining professionalism can help you stay above unproductive political maneuverings.

Managing relationships strategically in the workplace can minimize the impact of office politics. Building positive relationships with many colleagues, including those in key positions, can help navigate political situations more effectively.

Recognizing and avoiding time wasters is essential. This might involve declining unnecessary meetings, minimizing time spent on unproductive activities, and setting clear boundaries to protect your time.

Staying focused on your goals and responsibilities can help you navigate office politics and time wasters. Keeping your objectives in mind and prioritizing tasks that contribute to these goals can help you stay on track.

Seeking mentorship or advice from experienced colleagues can provide insights into effectively navigating office politics and managing time wasters. Learning from others' experiences can be invaluable in developing your own strategies.

Maintaining a positive and professional attitude in the face of office politics and time wasters is important. A positive outlook can help you navigate these challenges more effectively and maintain your focus on your work.

INTEGRATING WORK AND PERSONAL LIFE

Achieving a balance between work and personal life is essential for overall well-being and effective time management. Striking this balance involves setting boundaries, prioritizing, and finding synergy between work and personal responsibilities.

Setting clear boundaries between work and personal life helps prevent one from encroaching on the other. This might involve specific work hours, turning off work notifications outside of these hours, or having distinct spaces for work and relaxation.

Prioritizing self-care and personal commitments is as important as work responsibilities. Allocating time for hobbies, family, friends, and relaxation ensures a well-rounded life and can actually enhance work performance by reducing burnout and increasing satisfaction.

Finding ways to integrate work and personal life can make balancing the two more achievable. This might involve flexible work hours that accommodate personal commitments or bringing elements of personal interests into your work.

Communicating your needs and boundaries to employers, colleagues, and family is key. Open and honest communication helps manage expectations and find support for maintaining a work-life balance.

Regularly assessing your work-life balance and making adjustments as needed is important. As your personal and professional circumstances change, so too might your approach to balancing these aspects of your life.

Embracing flexibility and adaptability in balancing work and personal life is crucial. Being open to adjusting your approach in response to changing circumstances can help you maintain a balance that works for you.

EVOLVING WITH CHANGING WORK TRENDS

In the ever-shifting landscape of modern work, adaptability and openness to change are vital for effective time management. Adapting to technological advancements, shifts in work practices, or industry trends is crucial for enhancing both productivity and career growth.

Keeping abreast of industry trends and developments can give you an edge in your field. Regular engagement with industry publications, webinars or conferences, and peer networking are effective ways to stay informed and ahead.

Embracing new technologies and working methodologies can lead to improved efficiency and new career avenues. Whether mastering new software, adapting to remote working conditions, or adopting innovative work strategies, openness to change can significantly boost your skillset and efficiency.

Cultivating a mindset geared towards continuous learning is critical to keeping pace with the ever-changing work environment. This entails a dedication to ongoing professional development and an eagerness to learn and adapt continuously.

Actively seeking opportunities to apply new skills and knowledge reinforces learning and enhances your adaptability. Engage in projects or roles where you can utilize your new skills, whether in your current position, through side projects, or volunteer activities.

Building a diverse network across various sectors and industries can offer valuable insights into evolving work trends. Networking provides different perspectives and opportunities to learn from the experiences and expertise of others.

Periodically reassessing and updating your career plans in response to changes in the work environment is crucial. As the professional landscape transforms, so should your career goals and strategies. Flexibility to reevaluate and modify your plans ensures they stay relevant and aligned with your personal ambitions and the prevailing professional climate.

TIME MANAGEMENT FOR CREATIVES

avigating the intricacies of time management in creative fields presents unique challenges and opportunities. This chapter explores how creatives can effectively manage their time, foster creativity within constraints, handle projects, overcome blocks, balance the demands of artistic professions, leverage collaboration and networking, integrate new technologies, and sustain a long-term creative career. These strategies are tailored to creative work's unique rhythms and requirements, ensuring that time management supports rather than stifles creative expression.

FOSTERING CREATIVITY WITHIN TIME CONSTRAINTS

Creativity often thrives within constraints, and setting time boundaries can actually enhance rather than inhibit creative work. Time constraints can foster focus, encourage decision-making, and spur innovative thinking under pressure.

Balancing structured time with unstructured creative explorations is critical. Structured time can be used for specific tasks like administrative work or meetings, while unstructured time allows for creative exploration without the pressure of deadlines.

Setting realistic deadlines for creative work helps manage expectations and maintain a productive workflow. While creativity cannot be forced, having a timeline provides a framework for channeling creative efforts.

Breaking creative work into smaller, manageable tasks can help work within time constraints. This approach allows for progress in increments, making large projects less daunting and more achievable.

Using time constraints as a creative tool involves embracing them as part of the process. Constraints can lead to new ways of thinking and push creatives to explore beyond their usual boundaries.

Flexibility in adjusting time constraints is important. While deadlines can be helpful, being open to adjusting them as needed allows for the organic nature of the creative process to unfold.

Regular reflection on how time constraints impact creativity can lead to better time management strategies. Understanding when constraints aid creativity and hinder it can help find the right balance in future projects.

MANAGING TIME IN CREATIVE PROJECTS

Effective time management in creative projects involves a balance between the organic flow of creativity and the practical aspects of project completion. This balance ensures that creative integrity is maintained while meeting deadlines and other constraints.

Prioritizing tasks within creative projects helps focus efforts where they are most needed. Distinguishing between high-priority creative tasks and less critical activities can optimize time use and ensure key project elements receive the attention they deserve.

Breaking projects into phases, or stages, can aid in time management. This approach allows for focusing on one aspect of the project at a time, reducing overwhelm and providing a clear path of progression.

Setting regular check-ins or milestones within a project can keep it on track. These check-ins are opportunities to assess progress, make adjustments, and ensure that the project is progressing as planned.

Balancing solo creative work with collaborative tasks is crucial. While individual work allows for a deep focus on creative tasks, collaboration brings new ideas and perspectives that can enhance the project.

Time tracking can be a valuable tool in managing creative projects. Monitoring how time is spent can provide insights into work patterns and help identify areas where efficiency can be improved.

Celebrating milestones within a project can boost motivation and creativity. Recognizing the completion of project stages reinforces progress and provides encouragement for the subsequent phases of work.

OVERCOMING CREATIVE BLOCKS

Creative blocks are a common challenge in creative professions. Overcoming these blocks involves a combination of strategies that foster inspiration and allow for a return to productive work.

Stepping away from the work can sometimes be the best way to overcome a block. Taking a break, engaging in a different activity, or simply changing the environment can provide a fresh perspective and spark new ideas.

Experimenting with different creative techniques or mediums can break the monotony and stimulate new ways of thinking. Trying new methods can lead to unexpected breakthroughs and reignite creativity.

Seeking inspiration from other sources, such as art, nature, literature, or even unrelated fields, can provide fresh ideas and perspectives to help overcome creative blocks.

Setting aside specific times for brainstorming or free-form exploration can provide a safe space for creativity without the pressure of immediate results. These sessions can lead to new ideas or solutions to creative challenges.

Collaborating with others can provide new insights and inspiration. Sharing ideas and getting feedback can open up new avenues for creative exploration.

Maintaining regular creative practice, even during periods of blockage, can keep the creative muscles active. Consistency in creative work, even in small doses, can eventually lead to a breakthrough.

Reflecting on past experiences of overcoming creative blocks can provide insights and strategies for dealing with current challenges. Understanding what has worked in the past can give insight into solutions to current creative obstacles.

TIME MANAGEMENT IN ARTISTIC PROFESSIONS

Time management in artistic professions requires balancing creative work with the practicalities of a professional career. This balance ensures that artistic pursuits are sustainable and that the practical aspects of an artistic career are managed effectively.

Developing a routine that accommodates both creative work and administrative tasks is essential. A structured routine ensures that both creative and practical tasks receive the necessary attention.

Allocating specific times for creative work can help maintain a consistent artistic practice. These dedicated creative periods allow for focused work without the distractions of other professional responsibilities.

Balancing artistic projects with income-generating work can be a challenge. It involves finding a balance between pursuing creative passions and fulfilling an artistic career's financial and practical requirements.

Time management strategies in artistic professions should be adaptable to the ebb and flow of creative work. Being flexible in scheduling and prioritizing tasks allows for natural fluctuations in creative energy and inspiration.

Networking and promotional activities are important aspects of an artistic career. Allocating time for these activities ensures visibility and professional growth, crucial for sustaining an artistic career.

Reflecting on and adjusting time management strategies regularly ensures that they continue to meet the evolving needs of an artistic career. As artistic pursuits and professional opportunities change, so too should approaches to managing time.

LEVERAGING COLLABORATION AND NETWORKING

Collaboration and networking are key elements of successful creative careers. They provide opportunities for learning, inspiration, and professional growth, all of which contribute to effective time management in creative professions.

Collaborating with other creatives can lead to shared ideas, skills, and resources, making projects more efficient and innovative. It allows for pooling talents and dividing tasks, optimizing time use, and enhancing work quality.

Networking with professionals in your field and beyond can open up new opportunities and provide valuable insights. Regular engagement with a network of peers, mentors, and industry professionals can lead to collaborations, job opportunities, and new ideas.

Participating in collaborative projects can provide learning and growth opportunities. Working with others exposes you to new perspectives and techniques, which can enhance your own creative practice.

Effective networking involves both in-person and online interactions. Attending industry events, participating in online forums, and maintaining an active professional presence on social media can expand your network and open up new opportunities.

Balancing time spent on collaborative and networking activities with solo creative work is important. While collaboration and networking are valuable, they should complement rather than overshadow your individual creative practice.

Regular reflection on the value and impact of your collaborative and networking activities can help optimize their effectiveness. Assessing how these activities contribute to your creative and professional goals can guide future efforts in collaboration and networking.

INTEGRATING NEW TECHNOLOGIES

Staying abreast of and integrating new technologies is essential in modern creative professions. Technology can enhance creative possibilities, streamline processes, and open new avenues for artistic expression and professional growth.

Exploring and adopting new technologies that align with your creative work can enhance efficiency and expand your creative capabilities. Whether it's new software, digital tools, or emerging platforms, leveraging the right technology can transform your creative process.

Balancing the use of technology with traditional creative methods is key. While technology offers new possibilities, it should complement, rather than replace, the fundamental aspects of your creative practice.

Using technology to streamline administrative and promotional tasks can free up more time for creative work.

Automation tools, digital marketing platforms, and online project management systems can reduce the time spent on non-creative tasks.

Staying informed about technological trends and developments in your field can give you a competitive edge. Regularly exploring industry news, attending workshops, and engaging with professional networks can keep you updated on relevant technologies.

Experimenting with different technologies can lead to innovative and creative work. Trying new tools and methods can open up new possibilities and inspire fresh ideas and approaches.

Reflecting on the impact of technology on your creative work and professional efficiency is important. Regularly assessing how technology tools and platforms contribute to your work can guide future decisions on technology integration.

SUSTAINING A LONG-TERM CREATIVE CAREER

Maintaining a creative career over the long term requires a delicate balance between creative satisfaction, professional advancement, and personal well-being. Effective time management is pivotal in achieving this equilibrium and ensuring a sustainable and rewarding journey in the creative field.

Crafting a career plan that harmoniously blends creative desires with pragmatic elements is vital. This plan should encompass your artistic objectives, income strategies, professional growth plans, and personal wellness considerations.

Continuously developing and honing your creative abilities is essential for long-term success. This means allocating time for ongoing education, creative exploration, and mastering your artistic discipline.

Diversifying your income sources is vital to financial stability and can provide greater creative liberty. Exploring various revenue channels, such as undertaking commissions, teaching, or selling products, can lay a more solid foundation for your creative pursuits.

Cultivating and nurturing a robust professional network is crucial for the longevity of your career. A strong network offers support, opens up opportunities, and creates a sense of community, all contributing to a lasting and satisfying creative journey.

Prioritizing self-care and personal health is just as important as focusing on professional growth. Allocating time for rest, relaxation, and personal interests is essential to prevent burnout and keep your creative spark alive.

Regular evaluations and adjustments to your career trajectory are important to remain aligned with your changing personal goals, industry shifts, and life circumstances. Staying flexible and receptive to change ensures that your creative path remains rewarding and attuned to your evolving aspirations and values.

TIME MANAGEMENT FOR ENTREPRENEURS

*E*ntrepreneurship requires a distinct approach to time *management, where the swift tempo of startup culture meets the necessities of strategic foresight and personal health. This chapter delves into the intricacies of effective time management for entrepreneurs. It covers various critical topics, including efficient task prioritization, striking a balance between innovation and practical implementation, honing delegation skills, managing time amidst business expansion, effective networking, strategically handling risks, and preserving personal well-being. The strategies outlined are tailored to assist entrepreneurs in tackling the complexities of their multifaceted roles, all while fostering enduring success and maintaining their health.*

PRIORITIZING IN A STARTUP ENVIRONMENT

In the fast-paced world of startups, prioritizing tasks is essential. Entrepreneurs often face a myriad of tasks each day, and knowing which ones to tackle first can significantly impact the success of the business.

The key to effective prioritization is identifying tasks that align closely with the startup's immediate goals and objectives. This might mean focusing on activities that drive growth, secure funding, or build essential infrastructure.

Urgent tasks often demand immediate attention, but it's important to distinguish between urgency and importance. Entrepreneurs must ensure that urgent tasks do not consistently overshadow important strategic initiatives that contribute to long-term success.

Adopting agile methodologies can be beneficial in startup environments. These approaches allow for quick adjustments based on immediate feedback and changing market conditions, which is crucial for startups.

Learning to say no to tasks or opportunities that do not align with the startup's core objectives is vital. Time is a limited resource, and being selective is critical to effective time management.

Regularly reviewing and adjusting priorities based on the startup's progress and market feedback ensures that efforts remain aligned with business needs. This flexibility is crucial in the dynamic startup environment.

Regular planning sessions, whether daily or weekly, help maintain focus on top priorities and ensure that time is allocated effectively across tasks.

BALANCING INNOVATION AND EXECUTION

For entrepreneurs, balancing the time spent on innovation with the time needed for execution is crucial. While innovation drives the startup forward, execution turns innovative ideas into reality and generates tangible results.

Allocating specific brainstorming and creative thinking times can ensure that innovation remains a core part of the startup's culture. This set aside time keeps day-to-day operational tasks from overshadowing innovation.

Translating innovative ideas into actionable plans is essential. Entrepreneurs need to ensure that time spent on innovation leads to concrete steps towards implementation.

Balancing risk-taking with practicality is a crucial aspect of managing innovation. While it's important to explore new ideas, entrepreneurs also need to assess their feasibility and potential impact on the business.

Involving the team in both the innovation and execution processes can lead to more comprehensive and effective strategies. Collaboration ensures diverse perspectives and skills are applied to both creative thinking and practical implementation.

Setting realistic timelines for implementing innovative ideas helps manage expectations and maintain momentum. It ensures that innovation is pursued in a structured and time-efficient manner.

Reflecting on the outcomes of innovation efforts, whether successful or not, provides valuable learning experiences. These reflections can guide future innovation strategies and execution plans.

EFFECTIVE DELEGATION AND LEADERSHIP

Effective delegation is a critical skill for entrepreneurs. It involves entrusting tasks to team members, freeing up time for strategic planning and business development.

Identifying tasks to delegate starts with understanding your strengths and weaknesses. Delegating tasks that others can do better or more efficiently allows entrepreneurs to focus on areas where they add the most value.

Clear communication when delegating tasks is essential. It ensures that team members understand their responsibilities, expectations, and the context of their tasks within the broader business goals.

Building a reliable team is key to effective delegation. This involves hiring skilled individuals and fostering a culture of trust and accountability.

Delegation also involves letting go of the need for control. Entrepreneurs need to trust their team's abilities and allow them to take ownership of tasks and projects.

Regular check-ins and feedback loops ensure that delegated tasks are on track and align with business objectives. These check-ins also provide opportunities for coaching and development.

Developing leadership skills, such as decision-making, communication, and emotional intelligence, enhances an entrepreneur's ability to manage time effectively and lead their business toward success.

TIME MANAGEMENT IN SCALING BUSINESSES

As businesses grow and scale, time management challenges evolve. Entrepreneurs need to adapt their strategies to manage a scaling business's increasing complexity and demands.

Strategic planning becomes even more critical during business scaling. Entrepreneurs need to allocate time to develop and refine growth strategies, ensuring that the business expands in a sustainable and controlled manner.

Effective systematization and process optimization can save significant time in scaling businesses. Implementing scalable systems and processes ensures that operations run efficiently and can accommodate growth.

Delegating operational responsibilities becomes increasingly important as the business grows. Entrepreneurs need to empower their management team to handle day-to-day operations, allowing them to focus on strategic growth.

Time management during scaling also involves identifying and focusing on key growth drivers. Concentrating efforts on areas with the highest growth potential ensures efficient use of time and resources.

Managing time effectively during scaling often requires seeking external advice and guidance. Advisors, mentors, or consultants with experience in scaling businesses can provide valuable insights and strategies.

Reflecting on and learning from each stage of business growth is important. Understanding what worked and what didn't at each stage can guide future growth strategies and time management approaches.

NETWORKING AND RELATIONSHIP BUILDING

For entrepreneurs, networking and building relationships are essential activities that require strategic time management. These connections can open doors to new opportunities, partnerships, and resources.

Allocating specific times for networking activities ensures that they are not neglected amid other business demands. Whether attending industry events, participating in online forums, or scheduling one-on-one meetings, dedicated time for networking is crucial.

Building meaningful relationships takes time and effort. Entrepreneurs should focus on quality over quantity in their networking efforts, developing deeper connections that are mutually beneficial.

Leveraging social media and professional platforms for networking can be time-efficient. These platforms provide opportunities to connect with a broader audience and engage with industry peers and potential partners.

Following up and maintaining connections is as important as making initial contacts. Regular communication, whether through emails, calls, or meetings, helps nurture these relationships over time.

Balancing networking activities with other business responsibilities is critical. Entrepreneurs need to ensure that time spent on networking is productive and contributes to the business's growth and objectives.

Reflecting on the value of networking and relationship-building efforts can guide future strategies. Assessing the impact of these activities on the business can help determine how best to allocate time and resources to them in the future.

RISK MANAGEMENT AND TIME ALLOCATION

Effective risk management is a critical aspect of entrepreneurship, directly impacting how time is allocated. Entrepreneurs must identify potential risks to their business and allocate time to develop strategies to mitigate these risks.

Conducting regular risk assessments helps identify potential challenges that could impact the business. This proactive approach allows entrepreneurs to allocate time to address these risks before they become larger issues.

Developing contingency plans for identified risks ensures that the business can continue operating smoothly in the face of challenges. These plans should be reviewed and updated regularly to remain effective.

Allocating time to monitor market trends and industry changes helps anticipate and manage risks. Staying informed allows entrepreneurs to adjust their strategies in response to external factors.

Balancing risk management with opportunity pursuit is crucial. While it's important to be cautious, entrepreneurs must also allocate time to explore new opportunities that could benefit the business.

Incorporating risk management into the business culture and processes ensures that it becomes an integral part of the business's operations. This approach fosters a mindset of proactive risk management among the entire team.

Reflecting on past experiences with risks and their management can provide valuable lessons. These reflections can inform future risk management strategies and time allocation decisions.

SUSTAINING PERSONAL WELL-BEING

For entrepreneurs, maintaining personal well-being is a cornerstone of achieving lasting success. Juggling the demands of entrepreneurship can be intense, and overlooking personal health can result in burnout and diminished efficiency.

Carving out time for self-care, including physical activities, hobbies, or relaxation, is essential. These activities are vital for preserving both physical and mental health and coping with entrepreneurship's rigors.

Finding a balance between professional obligations and personal life is fundamental for overall well-being. Entrepreneurs should dedicate time to their business endeavors, family, friends, and personal interests.

Adopting mindfulness and stress-reduction techniques can be instrumental in managing entrepreneurial pressures. Practices like meditation, deep breathing, or yoga offer essential mental respite and can boost focus and productivity.

Regular health check-ups and paying attention to physical well-being are critical. Entrepreneurs need to prioritize their health and seek medical care when necessary to ensure they can run their businesses effectively.

Seeking support from mentors, coaches, or peer groups provides emotional backing and practical insights. This network of support can be a crucial asset in tackling the challenges of entrepreneurship.

Periodic reflection on personal well-being and making necessary adjustments is crucial. Regularly assessing the impact of entrepreneurial endeavors on personal health and happiness can inform changes in work habits and lifestyle choices.

TIME MANAGEMENT FOR STUDENTS

ime management in a student's life involves juggling academic responsibilities, part-time work, and social engagements; mastering efficient study methods; gearing up for examinations; engaging in extracurricular activities; charting future career paths; utilizing technology effectively; and cultivating a strong support network. This chapter provides guidance and tactics specifically designed to address the distinct challenges faced by students. It aims to assist them in efficiently traversing their academic path while laying the groundwork for their future achievements.

BALANCING ACADEMICS, WORK, AND SOCIAL LIFE

Achieving a balance between academics, work, and social life is critical to student life. This balance is crucial to maintaining well-being and ensuring success in all areas.

Prioritizing academic responsibilities is essential, but allocating time for part-time work and social activities is also important. Striking this balance requires careful planning and an understanding of one's own limits and capacities.

Creating a schedule that includes classes, study time, work hours, and social activities can help manage time effectively. This schedule should be realistic, allowing flexibility to accommodate unexpected changes or opportunities.

Setting clear boundaries between study, work, and leisure time helps prevent burnout. This involves dedicating specific times for each activity and being mindful not to let one area encroach upon another.

Learning to say no to activities or commitments that overload the schedule is important. While taking on every opportunity is tempting, overcommitting can lead to stress and reduced performance.

Using downtime effectively, such as socializing to allow for relaxation and rejuvenation, can enhance overall balance. The quality, rather than quantity, of social time often leads to more fulfilling experiences.

Regularly reassessing how well the balance is working and making adjustments as needed ensures that the approach remains effective. This ongoing assessment helps respond to changing circumstances and maintain a healthy balance.

EFFECTIVE STUDY TECHNIQUES

Effective study techniques are crucial for academic success and efficient use of time. Developing and honing these techniques can lead to better learning outcomes and more manageable study schedules.

Active learning strategies can enhance understanding and retention, such as summarizing information in your own words, teaching concepts to others, or applying theories to practical examples.

Creating a dedicated study space, free from distractions, aids concentration and productivity. This space should be conducive to learning, equipped with the necessary materials, and have a comfortable setup.

Using a variety of study methods keeps the learning process engaging. Alternating between reading, writing, visual aids, and interactive tools caters to different learning styles and prevents monotony.

Breaking study sessions into manageable time blocks with short breaks in between, known as the Pomodoro Technique, can enhance focus and prevent fatigue.

Setting specific goals for each study session helps keep you on track. Clear objectives ensure that time is spent productively and key topics or assignments are covered.

Regularly reviewing and revising study materials reinforces learning. This ongoing revision consolidates knowledge and reduces the need for last-minute cramming.

Seeking help when needed, whether from teachers, tutors, or peers, can clarify difficult concepts and save time. Understanding material correctly from the start prevents confusion and time wasted on incorrect assumptions.

MANAGING TIME FOR EXAMS AND DEADLINES

Managing time effectively for exams and deadlines is a critical skill for students. It involves planning, prioritization, and disciplined study habits.

Developing a study schedule well in advance of exams or deadlines can ensure adequate preparation. This timetable should allocate time based on the complexity of subjects and personal strengths and weaknesses.

Prioritizing subjects or topics that require more attention or are more challenging helps in efficiently using study time. Focusing on these areas ensures that they receive the necessary time and effort.

Using past exams or assignments as practice can help in understanding the format and types of questions to expect. This practice also aids in time management during the actual exam or project completion.

Balancing the depth and breadth of study is important. While it's necessary to cover all topics, diving too deeply into one area at the expense of others can be counterproductive.

Taking care of physical and mental health during exam preparations is crucial. Regular exercise, healthy eating, and adequate sleep enhance cognitive function and overall performance.

Reflecting on each exam or project after completion can provide insights for future time management strategies. Assessing what worked well and what could be improved helps refine approaches for subsequent exams and deadlines.

TIME MANAGEMENT IN EXTRACURRICULAR ACTIVITIES

Engaging in extracurricular activities can significantly enhance the student's experience. Yet managing time to balance these activities with academic duties is crucial.

Selecting extracurriculars that resonate with your personal passions and career ambitions can make the time invested in them both enjoyable and significant. This careful selection ensures that these activities enrich personal development and align with future goals.

Striking a balance between time spent on extracurriculars and academic tasks demands strategic planning. Designating specific times for each and ensuring that neither dominates the other is essential for achieving equilibrium.

Utilizing extracurricular pursuits to cultivate skills such as time management, leadership, and teamwork offers invaluable learning opportunities. These competencies are versatile, serving students well in their academic journey and future professional endeavors.

Opting for extracurricular activities judiciously helps you avoid overextending yourself. Concentrating on a few chosen activities that truly matter can lead to a more rewarding and manageable level of involvement.

Incorporating social elements into extracurriculars can simultaneously address social needs and engage in constructive activities. This approach allows for a well-rounded extracurricular experience.

Periodic evaluation of how extracurricular activities affect your time management and overall student life is vital. Such assessments are crucial to making informed choices about continuing, adjusting, or ceasing participation in specific activities.

PLANNING FOR FUTURE CAREERS AND GOALS

Planning for future careers and goals is an integral part of time management for students. This planning involves setting career objectives, acquiring relevant skills, and aligning academic pursuits with future aspirations.

Identifying career interests and goals early in the academic journey helps make informed decisions about courses, majors, and extracurricular activities. This clarity guides time management decisions and ensures that efforts are aligned with long-term objectives.

Seeking internships, part-time jobs, or volunteer opportunities in fields of interest provides practical experience and insight into potential career paths. These experiences can guide future career decisions and provide a competitive edge.

Networking with professionals in desired industries or fields can provide valuable insights and connections. Allocating time for networking, whether through formal events or informal interactions, can open doors to future opportunities.

Using academic projects or assignments to explore areas of career interest can enhance learning and contribute to career goals. This approach provides practical experience in areas of interest and can be a valuable addition to a resume or portfolio.

Regularly revisiting and adjusting career plans based on experiences, feedback, and changing interests ensures that plans remain relevant and inspiring. Flexibility in career planning allows for exploration and adaptation to new opportunities or insights.

Reflecting on the skills and competencies required for desired career paths can guide academic and extracurricular choices. Focusing on developing these skills ensures that time spent in academic and extracurricular activities contributes effectively to future career goals.

LEVERAGING TECHNOLOGY FOR ACADEMIC EFFICIENCY

Technology can be a powerful tool for enhancing academic efficiency and time management. Leveraging the right technological tools can streamline study processes, enhance learning, and save time.

Using educational apps and software for organizing study materials, tracking assignments, and managing deadlines can significantly enhance academic efficiency. These tools provide a centralized platform for managing academic responsibilities.

Online resources, such as educational videos, tutorials, and academic databases, can supplement traditional learning materials and provide diverse perspectives on subjects. These resources can be time-efficient ways to enhance understanding and deepen knowledge.

Utilizing digital note-taking and organization tools can streamline the process of note-taking and study material review. Digital tools allow for easy organization, searchability, and access to notes and resources.

Participating in online study groups or forums can provide peer support and additional learning resources. These platforms offer opportunities for collaborative learning and the sharing of ideas and resources.

Balancing the use of technology with traditional study methods is important. While technology offers many benefits, engaging in offline study practices that suit individual learning styles is crucial.

Regularly evaluating the effectiveness of technology tools and strategies in academic work ensures that they continue to meet learning needs. As technology evolves and academic demands change, reassessing and adapting technology use is key to maintaining academic efficiency.

BUILDING SUPPORT NETWORKS

Establishing a robust support network is crucial for students, offering a foundation of emotional backing, academic help, and career advice. These networks play a crucial role in efficiently managing time and overcoming the various hurdles of student life.

Building a network comprising peers, mentors, and advisors brings a wide array of support and differing viewpoints. Peers provide a sense of camaraderie and opportunity for collaboration; mentors offer wisdom and counsel; and advisors aid in academic and career direction.

Getting involved in student groups, clubs, or study circles broadens your network. These communities create avenues to connect with others who share similar interests and can provide academic and personal support.

Seeking mentors, such as faculty members, professionals in your field of interest, or senior students, can yield invaluable insights and advice. Mentors can share wisdom from their own experiences, assisting in academic and career choices.

Utilizing university resources like counseling, academic advising, and career services offers specialized support in managing academic duties, career planning, and personal challenges.

Cultivating relationships with professors or instructors is also advantageous. These connections can offer academic guidance and potentially lead to research opportunities or professional networking.

Regular interaction with and nurturing of your support network is essential for its effectiveness. Maintaining consistent communication and active participation in network activities ensures the strength and reliability of these relationships.

TIME MANAGEMENT FOR PARENTS

or parents, adept time management is key to both nurturing their family and preserving their own well-being. This chapter tackles the multifaceted task of juggling parental duties with personal time. It covers balancing the demands of parenting with individual needs, creating efficient family routines, scheduling children's activities, navigating parenthood in the era of digital technology, emphasizing the importance of self-care, teaching children about managing their time, and strategizing for the family's future. These approaches are crafted to assist parents in overcoming the hurdles of parenthood, ensuring a rewarding family experience and personal development.

BALANCING PARENTING AND PERSONAL TIME

Achieving a balance between parenting and personal time is essential for parents' overall well-being and effectiveness. This balance allows for fulfilling family responsibilities while also maintaining individual identity and interests.

Setting aside dedicated time for personal interests and hobbies is crucial. This personal time can provide a much-needed break from parenting duties, offering a chance to recharge and pursue personal growth.

Effective communication with partners or co-parents about time needs and expectations can aid in balancing parenting and personal responsibilities. This open dialogue helps in understanding each other's needs and in creating a supportive environment.

Creating boundaries between parenting time and personal time is important. Whether setting specific hours for personal activities or having designated 'me time,' these boundaries help maintain a healthy balance.

Balancing parenting and personal time often require flexibility and adaptability. Parents need to be prepared to adjust their schedules and plans based on the evolving needs of their family and personal lives.

Enlisting the support of family, friends, or childcare services can provide parents with the time needed for personal pursuits. This support network can be invaluable in maintaining a balance between parenting and personal time.

Reflecting regularly on the balance between parenting and personal time and making adjustments as needed ensures that both aspects of life receive the necessary attention and focus.

EFFECTIVE ROUTINES FOR FAMILIES

Establishing effective routines can significantly enhance a family's time management. Routines provide structure and predictability, which can be especially beneficial for children, creating a sense of security and stability.

Morning and evening routines are particularly important in setting the tone for the day and ensuring a smooth transition to bedtime. These routines can include activities like family breakfasts, preparing for the day, and bedtime stories.

Involving children in creating and maintaining family routines can encourage cooperation and responsibility. It also allows them to learn time management skills and understand the importance of routines.

Balancing structured routines with flexibility is critical. While routines are beneficial, being too rigid can lead to stress, especially when unexpected situations arise. Flexibility allows the family to adapt to changes while maintaining a sense of routine.

Regularly reviewing and adjusting family routines based on the family's evolving needs and circumstances ensures that they remain practical and relevant. This review can consider schedule changes, children's developmental stages, and family goals.

Allocating time within routines for family bonding activities, such as shared meals or game nights, strengthens family relationships and creates cherished memories.

Effective routines also include time for chores and household responsibilities. Distributing these tasks among family members according to their age and ability can teach responsibility and teamwork.

MANAGING TIME FOR CHILDREN'S ACTIVITIES

Managing time for children's activities involves balancing their developmental needs with other family commitments. This balance ensures that children engage in enriching activities without overburdening the family schedule.

Prioritizing activities based on their value and impact on children's growth helps in making informed decisions about which activities to pursue. This prioritization involves considering the benefits of each activity in terms of social, educational, and physical development.

Setting realistic limits on the number of activities children are involved in prevents overscheduling. Too many activities can lead to stress for both children and parents and diminish each activity's enjoyment and benefits.

Coordinating activities with other parents or carpooling can save time and effort. Sharing transportation duties or arranging joint activities can be efficient ways to manage time and resources.

Incorporating downtime into children's schedules is important. Unstructured time allows children to relax, play freely, and develop creativity and imagination.

Being present and engaged during children's activities, rather than multitasking, can enhance the experience for both the child and the parent. This presence fosters stronger bonds and creates meaningful experiences.

Regularly reassessing the schedule of children's activities based on their interests, feedback, and family dynamics ensures that their extracurricular involvement remains enjoyable and beneficial.

PARENTING IN THE DIGITAL AGE

Parenting in the digital age presents unique challenges and opportunities in time management. Navigating the use of technology in children's lives requires careful consideration and planning.

Setting guidelines for technology use, including screen time limits and appropriate content, helps manage children's engagement with digital devices. These guidelines should be age-appropriate and consistently enforced.

Balancing technology use with offline activities is crucial. Encouraging children to engage in physical play, outdoor activities, and face-to-face social interactions ensures a well-rounded development.

Staying informed about the latest digital trends and potential risks helps parents effectively guide their children's technology use. This knowledge enables parents to have informed discussions with their children about safe and responsible technology use.

Using technology as a tool for learning and development can be beneficial. Educational apps, online resources, and interactive games can supplement traditional learning methods and engage children in various subjects.

Leading by example in the use of technology is important. Parents' own habits with technology set a precedent for children. Demonstrating balanced and mindful use of technology can positively influence children's digital habits.

Open communication about technology and its benefits and drawbacks encourages a healthy relationship with digital devices. Regular discussions about technology use can help children understand its role and limits in their lives.

SELF-CARE FOR PARENTS

Self-care is a pivotal component of effective parenting. By attending to their own physical, emotional, and mental health, parents are better equipped to care for their children and set an example of healthy living practices.

Making self-care a priority, with activities like exercise, engaging in hobbies, or practicing relaxation methods, is vital. Consistently dedicating time to these pursuits can alleviate stress, uplift spirits, and bolster overall health.

It's also essential for parents to seek support when necessary, be it from relatives, friends, support circles, or professional services. Parenting presents its own set of challenges, and a solid support system offers both emotional solace and hands-on help.

Allocating dedicated time for self-care should be a steadfast fixture in one's schedule. This dedicated time is as crucial as any other commitment and is fundamental for sustaining personal health and resilience.

Balancing self-care with the responsibilities of parenting may call for inventive solutions. Weaving self-care into everyday life or including children in these activities can help integrate self-care more seamlessly into a parent's routine.

It's also imperative for parents to stay vigilant for burnout symptoms and take action when necessary. Acknowledging the need for rest and addressing stress proactively is key to maintaining both personal well-being and the ability to parent effectively.

Regular evaluation and adaptation of self-care routines ensure that these practices remain effective and aligned with individual needs, guaranteeing that self-care continues to be a central and fruitful aspect of a parent's life.

EDUCATING CHILDREN ON TIME MANAGEMENT

Teaching children time management skills is a valuable aspect of parenting. These skills help children develop responsibility, independence, and the ability to prioritize and organize their activities.

Introducing basic time management concepts, such as schedules and routines, in age-appropriate ways can lay the foundation for these skills. This introduction can involve simple tasks like following a daily routine or using a basic calendar.

Involving children in planning and decision-making helps them understand the concept of time management. This involvement can include letting them help plan their weekly activities or decide on their study schedule.

Teaching children to set their own goals and priorities helps develop their decision-making and time-management skills. Encouraging them to think about what they want to achieve and how to allocate their time effectively fosters independence and responsibility.

Using tools like timers, planners, or apps can aid children in managing their time. These tools can make the concept of time more tangible and help children plan and track their activities.

Leading by example in time management practices is crucial. Children often mimic the behaviors they observe, so demonstrating effective time management in your own life can positively influence their habits.

Regularly discussing time management with children and providing guidance and support helps reinforce these skills. These discussions can involve reviewing how they spend their time, offering suggestions, and celebrating their successes in managing their time effectively.

FAMILY PLANNING AND FUTURE GOALS

Planning for the family's future and setting collective goals is an important aspect of time management for parents. This planning involves considering the family's long-term aspirations and aligning current actions and decisions with these objectives.

Whether related to finances, education, travel, or lifestyle, setting family goals helps guide family decisions and activities. These goals provide direction and purpose for the family's collective efforts.

Involving all family members in the planning process fosters a sense of teamwork and shared responsibility. This involvement can include discussing goals, making decisions together, and setting collective objectives.

Regular family meetings to discuss plans and track progress can enhance communication and ensure that everyone is aligned with the family's goals. These meetings provide an opportunity for open discussion and collective decision-making.

Balancing individual family members' needs and aspirations with collective goals is key. Ensuring that each member's personal goals and interests are considered and respected is important for maintaining harmony and support within the family.

Planning for major life events, such as children's education, career changes, or retirement, requires foresight and careful consideration. Allocating time to discuss and prepare for these events ensures that the family is ready for future milestones.

Reflecting on and adjusting family plans and goals based on changes in circumstances, priorities, or interests ensures that the family's plans remain relevant and meaningful. Regular reassessment allows the family to adapt and grow together, ensuring that their collective journey is fulfilling and aligned with their evolving aspirations.

ADVANCED TIME MANAGEMENT TECHNIQUES

This chapter explores sophisticated strategies for those aiming to refine their time management skills, enhancing their efficiency and productivity. It includes learning how to use time management tools and apps well, fine-tuning workflows for peak performance, figuring out why people put things off and how to stop them, managing time in high-stress situations, making sure that time management strategies are in line with overall life goals, and encouraging a culture of always getting better and being flexible. Additionally, it advocates for a holistic perspective on time management. These advanced techniques are intended to offer an enriched understanding and a more subtle execution of time management fundamentals, assisting individuals not just in optimizing their time but also in ensuring their time investment aligns with their wider life ambitions.

MASTERING TIME MANAGEMENT TOOLS AND APPS

The proficient use of time management tools and apps can significantly enhance efficiency and organization. Selecting tools that align with personal working styles and needs is crucial for their effectiveness.

Exploring various tools and apps, from digital calendars and task managers to project management software, can help identify the most suitable options. Experimentation is key to finding the tools that resonate with individual preferences and work requirements.

Customizing tools to fit specific needs can further enhance their effectiveness. Many apps offer customization options that allow users to tailor features to their particular workflow and preferences.

Integrating various tools to create a cohesive system can streamline processes and improve time management. For example, syncing a digital calendar with a task management app can provide a comprehensive overview of schedules and to-dos.

Staying updated on new features and updates for chosen tools ensures that their benefits are maximized. Regularly exploring new functionalities can lead to more efficient use and better time management outcomes.

Training and practice are essential for mastering these tools. Investing time in learning how to use them effectively can save significant time in the long run.

Reflecting on the effectiveness of these tools in managing time and making adjustments as needed ensures that they continue to meet changing needs and preferences.

OPTIMIZING WORKFLOWS FOR PEAK EFFICIENCY

Optimizing workflows involves analyzing and refining processes to achieve maximum efficiency. This optimization requires a thorough understanding of current workflows and an openness to change and improvement.

Identifying bottlenecks or inefficiencies in current processes is the first step in workflow optimization. This analysis can reveal areas where time is being wasted or where processes can be streamlined.

Implementing automation where possible can significantly increase efficiency. Automating repetitive or time-consuming tasks frees up time for more complex and rewarding work.

Developing a systematic approach to tasks can enhance productivity. This might involve standardizing procedures, creating templates, or establishing clear guidelines for recurring tasks.

Regularly reviewing and updating workflows in response to changing circumstances or new information ensures that they remain efficient and effective.

Balancing speed with quality is crucial to optimizing workflows. While efficiency is important, it should not come at the cost of the quality of work.

Involving team members in the optimization process can provide valuable insights and foster a culture of continuous improvement.

THE PSYCHOLOGY OF PROCRASTINATION AND OVERCOMING IT

Delving into the psychological roots of procrastination reveals that it's often more complex than a mere lapse in time management—it's frequently intertwined with deeper emotional or psychological challenges.

Identifying what prompts you to procrastinate, such as a fear of failure, the pursuit of perfection, or an absence of motivation, is critical to tackling the underlying issues. Recognizing these catalysts is the preliminary step toward crafting effective countermeasures.

Establishing minor, attainable objectives can act as a deterrent to procrastination. Such goals foster a sense of progress and momentum, rendering overwhelming tasks more approachable.

Cultivating a work setting that boosts motivation and curtails distractions can help diminish the propensity to procrastinate. This may involve organizing your work area, minimizing disruptions, or creating an environment conducive to productivity.

Deconstructing tasks into smaller, more digestible segments can make them appear less daunting and curb the impulse to delay. This strategy enables incremental advancement and mitigates the anxiety associated with large-scale projects.

Implementing a system of rewards for task completion can serve as a further impetus to counteract procrastination. Self-rewarding for achieving specific goals or milestones can forge a cycle of positive reinforcement.

Reflecting on the repercussions of procrastination and its influence on your goals and overall well-being can galvanize a commitment to behavioral change. Recognizing the adverse outcomes of delaying action can motivate a shift towards more proficient time management practices.

TIME MANAGEMENT IN HIGH-PRESSURE ENVIRONMENTS

Navigating time management in high-pressure scenarios requires sophisticated tactics to sustain productivity while mitigating stress. Such environments typically necessitate rapid decision-making, streamlined workflows, and adept prioritization under duress.

Honing the skill to evaluate and order tasks swiftly based on their urgency and significance is vital in tense situations. Mastering this ability enables you to concentrate on the most critical tasks pertinent to your immediate circumstances.

Retaining a composed and focused demeanor is key to managing time efficiently when under pressure. Employing methods like deep breathing, mindfulness, or taking brief pauses for composure can aid in maintaining mental clarity and focus.

In high-stress contexts, effective communication with team members or colleagues is fundamental. Ensuring communication is clear and to the point helps align team efforts and facilitates the efficient execution of tasks.

Fostering resilience to stress through consistent self-care and stress management practices can significantly improve your capacity to manage time effectively in high-pressure situations.

Reflecting on previous experiences in high-stress environments and analyzing successful and unsuccessful strategies can guide future time management approaches in similar contexts.

Establishing backup plans for unexpected developments can conserve time and alleviate stress in high-pressure conditions. Being equipped for various outcomes ensures effective time management, even when facing unforeseen challenges.

INTEGRATING TIME MANAGEMENT WITH LIFE GOALS

Integrating time management strategies with personal life goals ensures that time is spent in ways that are meaningful and aligned with long-term aspirations. This integration enhances a sense of purpose and fulfillment in how time is used.

Clearly defining personal and professional life goals provides direction for time management decisions. Knowing what you want to achieve in different areas of life helps you prioritize tasks and allocate time accordingly.

Aligning daily tasks and activities with broader life goals ensures that each day contributes to these larger objectives. This alignment helps in making decisions about how to spend time and what commitments to take on.

Regularly reviewing and adjusting time management strategies in light of life goals ensures that they remain relevant and effective. As goals evolve, so should time management approaches.

Balancing short-term tasks and long-term goals is key. While managing daily responsibilities is important, it's also crucial to allocate time to activities that contribute to long-term aspirations.

Reflecting on how well current time management practices are supporting life goals can guide adjustments and improvements. This reflection can reveal whether time is being spent in ways that align with and support these goals.

Seeking harmony between professional and personal aspirations in time management can lead to a more balanced and fulfilling life. Ensuring that time is allocated to both areas according to their importance and value can enhance overall satisfaction and achievement.

CONTINUOUS IMPROVEMENT AND ADAPTATION

Continuous improvement and adaptation in time management involve regularly evaluating and refining strategies to remain effective and responsive to changing circumstances. This approach ensures that time management techniques evolve and improve over time.

Embracing a mindset of continuous learning and openness to new methods can enhance time management skills. Being willing to try new techniques, learn from experiences, and adapt to new information is vital to ongoing improvement.

Regularly seeking feedback from others, whether colleagues, mentors, or family members, can provide new perspectives and insights into time management practices. This feedback can reveal areas for improvement and new strategies to consider.

Setting aside time for regular self-reflection and assessment of time management strategies helps identify improvement areas. This reflective practice allows for introspection and the conscious adaptation of time management techniques.

Staying informed about new time management trends, tools, and methodologies can provide opportunities for improvement and adaptation. Keeping abreast of developments in the field ensures that the most current and effective strategies are being used.

Experimenting with different approaches and being willing to change routines and habits can lead to more effective time management. Flexibility and a willingness to change are crucial for adapting to new situations and improving time management skills.

Measuring and tracking the effectiveness of time management strategies can provide concrete data for continuous improvement. Using tools like time trackers or productivity apps can help assess how well time management techniques are working and where adjustments are needed.

BEYOND TIME MANAGEMENT: A HOLISTIC APPROACH

Embracing a holistic approach to time management means looking beyond mere efficiency and considering its impact on overall well-being, contentment, and life quality. This perspective acknowledges that effective time management transcends productivity; it's about crafting a life that is both fulfilling and balanced.

It's essential to consider how time management affects physical and mental health. Practices that support overall health, including regular exercise, sufficient rest, and effective stress management, are fundamental to a holistic approach.

Achieving a balance between professional and personal life in time management decisions is crucial for a well-rounded life. Such equilibrium helps stave off burnout and maintains enthusiasm and satisfaction in both spheres of life.

Factoring in leisure and relaxation is as vital as considering work and productivity. Allocating time for hobbies, socializing, and relaxation is key to a more balanced and enjoyable lifestyle.

Understanding the significance of time beyond productivity is critical. Valuing moments spent with loved ones or in meaningful pursuits is important. Realizing that not all time needs to be productive in the conventional sense can lead to a richer use of time.

Reflecting on personal values and how they align with time management practices is necessary for ensuring that time is used in genuinely meaningful ways. This introspection aids in making choices that resonate with personal beliefs and objectives.

A holistic approach to time management is a constant balancing act among various life aspects. Regularly evaluating how time management techniques are supporting overall life goals and contentment can inform ongoing adjustments and enhancements.

THE FUTURE OF TIME
MANAGEMENT

*I*n this chapter, we journey through the future trajectory
of time management, delving into upcoming trends, its
connection with sustainable living practices, the influence of AI
and automation, the criticality of continuous learning, worldwide
viewpoints, the pursuit of balance between personal and professional life, and envisaging the future dynamics of work and lifestyle. These subjects provide a window into the potential evolution
and reshaping of time management in the face of technological
progress, shifting societal values, and individual goals, preparing
readers with the vision and flexibility needed for the future.

EMERGING TRENDS IN TIME MANAGEMENT

In an ever-evolving world, the methodologies for managing
time are also undergoing transformation. Keeping pace with
new trends is critical to remain effective and efficient in our
personal and professional lives.

A key emerging trend is the shift towards more flexible and adaptable time management methods. The once-standard nine-to-five schedule is becoming more fluid, making room for diverse life and work styles.

There's an increasing integration of mindfulness and overall well-being into time management. It's becoming clear that effective time management isn't just about efficiency; it's equally about dedicating time to mental health, relaxation, and self-care.

In our tech-saturated environment, digital detoxes and periods of disconnection are gaining importance in time management. Stepping away from screens is becoming a vital practice for maintaining focus and mitigating digital burnout.

The advent of remote and hybrid work models is redefining our approach to time management, merging work with personal life, and calling for innovative strategies to keep both realms productive and balanced.

Customization of time management tools through data analytics and user behavior insights is increasing, providing more personalized solutions for individual time management needs.

Lastly, there's an evolving emphasis on managing time-based on outcomes rather than mere task completion, highlighting the importance of the quality and impact of what we do with our time over the sheer volume of tasks accomplished.

INTEGRATING TIME MANAGEMENT WITH SUSTAINABLE LIVING

Sustainable living and time management are increasingly being viewed as interconnected concepts. Managing time effectively also involves considering the environmental and social impact of our daily choices and habits.

The concept of 'slow living' is gaining traction, advocating for a more deliberate and mindful approach to time, countering the culture of rush and overconsumption. This approach can lead to more sustainable lifestyle choices.

Time management strategies are being adapted to include sustainable practices, such as allocating time for activities like recycling, sustainable commuting, or supporting local businesses.

The balance between efficiency and sustainability is becoming a crucial consideration. This involves finding ways to manage time that are not only efficient but also environmentally and socially responsible.

Sustainable time management also involves being conscious of the long-term implications of our daily actions, both on personal well-being and the environment.

The trend towards minimalism in personal and professional life influences time management. Individuals can manage their time more sustainably and purposefully by focusing on what is truly important and reducing excess.

Educating oneself and others on the relationship between time management and sustainable living is becoming more important. This education can lead to more informed and conscious choices about how time is spent.

THE ROLE OF AI AND AUTOMATION

Artificial Intelligence (AI) and automation are rapidly transforming the landscape of time management. Their integration into daily life and work is reshaping how tasks are prioritized, scheduled, and executed.

AI is enabling more sophisticated and personalized time management tools. These tools can learn from user behavior and preferences to provide customized recommendations and optimizations.

Automating routine and repetitive tasks frees time for more complex and creative endeavors. This shift allows individuals and organizations to focus on high-value activities requiring human intelligence and creativity.

The challenge of managing the balance between automated and manual tasks is emerging. While automation brings efficiency, there's a need to maintain human touch and judgment in certain areas.

AI and automation also enable more effective project management and team collaboration, streamlining communication and coordination efforts.

There's a growing need to adapt to and learn new skills to effectively use AI and automation tools. Continuous learning and adaptation are becoming essential components of time management in the AI era.

Ethical considerations around AI and automation, including privacy and job displacement concerns, influence how these technologies are integrated into time management practices.

TIME MANAGEMENT FOR LIFELONG LEARNING

Lifelong learning is becoming increasingly important in a rapidly changing world. Effective time management is crucial to accommodating continuous learning throughout one's life.

Allocating regular time for learning and development, whether for professional advancement or personal enrichment, is becoming a key component of time management strategies.

The rise of online learning platforms and resources provides flexible and diverse learning opportunities. Managing time to take advantage of these resources is essential for ongoing personal and professional growth.

Balancing learning with other commitments requires strategic planning and prioritization. This balance ensures that learning is integrated seamlessly into daily life without overwhelming other responsibilities.

Learning how to learn efficiently, including mastering techniques like speed reading, memory enhancement, or focused study methods, is part of effective time management for lifelong learning.

Staying curious and open to new knowledge and skills is an important mindset. Cultivating this mindset ensures that lifelong learning is a continuous and enjoyable part of one's personal and professional journey.

Reflecting on and applying learning in practical contexts is crucial. This application ensures that the time invested in learning translates into tangible benefits and improvements in personal and professional life.

GLOBAL PERSPECTIVES ON TIME MANAGEMENT

Understanding time management from a global perspective involves recognizing and respecting the diverse cultural approaches to time. These varied perspectives can offer valuable insights and alternative strategies for managing time.

In some cultures, time is viewed as a linear and finite resource, leading to a more structured and scheduled approach to time management. In others, time is seen as more fluid, emphasizing flexibility and adaptability.

The concept of 'polychronic' versus 'monochronic' time orientation affects how people in different cultures manage time. Polychronic cultures often multitask and are more flexible with schedules, while monochronic cultures tend to focus on one task at a time and adhere strictly to schedules.

Understanding these cultural differences is important, especially in a globalized world where work and personal interactions often cross cultural boundaries. This understanding can lead to more effective communication and collaboration.

Adopting a global perspective on time management can lead to more innovative and effective strategies. Learning from different cultural approaches can enrich one's own time management practices.

Balancing respect for cultural differences with the demands of a globalized world is a crucial skill. Navigating these differences effectively can enhance both personal and professional interactions.

Reflecting on how cultural perspectives influence personal time management preferences and habits can provide deeper insights into one's own approach and potential areas for improvement.

PERSONAL AND PROFESSIONAL HARMONY

Achieving harmony between personal and professional life is an evolving aspect of time management. As the boundaries between work and personal life become increasingly blurred, finding a balance that supports both areas is crucial.

Integrating personal and professional goals can lead to a more holistic approach to time management. This integration ensures that time is allocated in ways that support overall life aspirations rather than just immediate tasks or responsibilities.

Setting boundaries between work and personal time is essential to maintaining this harmony. Clear boundaries help prevent work responsibilities from encroaching on personal time and vice versa.

Regular reflection on the balance between personal and professional life can guide adjustments to time management strategies. This reflection helps ensure that both areas are given the attention and time they deserve.

The rise of remote work and flexible working arrangements is reshaping the quest for personal and professional harmony. These changes offer opportunities to create more tailored and harmonious schedules.

Prioritizing activities that contribute to personal well-being and professional success can enhance this harmony. Activities like networking, skill development, or hobbies related to one's profession can serve dual purposes.

Seeking and maintaining a supportive environment at work and home is key to achieving this harmony. A supportive environment enables a more seamless integration of personal and professional responsibilities.

VISIONING THE FUTURE OF WORK AND LIFE

Anticipating the future of work and life means projecting how technological advances, societal shifts, and individual goals will redefine our time management strategies. This foresight is crucial for adapting to upcoming changes and trends.

The concept of work-life integration is becoming increasingly significant, suggesting a future where time management will embrace a more integrated approach to work and personal life, acknowledging their interrelation rather than treating them as separate entities.

Virtual and augmented reality advancements are poised to revolutionize our workspaces and time management approaches. These technologies promise novel collaboration, learning, and engagement methods, necessitating fresh time management tactics.

As mental health and well-being take center stage in workplace culture, they're likely to shape time management practices, making well-being activities an expected part of the work routine.

The idea of a four-day workweek and adaptable work hours is gaining popularity, challenging conventional time management standards and promoting a shift towards valuing productivity and well-being above strict work schedules.

Environmental and social responsibility are predicted to become more entrenched in our work and personal lives. Time management practices may increasingly account for sustainable actions and social engagements.

Preparing for the future involves remaining flexible and committed to ongoing learning and self-improvement. As the contours of work and life transform, our time management methods must evolve accordingly.

CONCLUSION: CONSOLIDATING TIME MASTERY FOR A FULFILLING LIFE

In this concluding section, we weave together the diverse elements of time mastery, pausing to reflect on the journey undertaken. We consider how mastering time management has enhanced life quality, delve into incorporating these practices into everyday routines, and discuss laying the groundwork for ongoing enhancement. Additionally, we explore how we can empower others through our understanding of time management, cast an eye toward the future of this essential skill, and conclude with some closing reflections on the importance of valuing and making the most of our time.

REFLECTING ON THE TIME MANAGEMENT JOURNEY

Reflecting on the journey of mastering time management is a crucial step in consolidating the lessons and strategies learned. This reflection allows for an appreciation of the progress made and the challenges overcome.

Looking back at the starting point of this journey can be enlightening. It provides insights into how perceptions and practices of time management have evolved and how they have impacted personal and professional life.

Assessing the changes in habits, routines, and attitudes toward time reveals the transformative power of effective time management. This transformation often leads to greater productivity, reduced stress, and a more balanced approach to life.

Celebrating successes, no matter how small, reinforces positive changes and boosts motivation to continue applying time management principles. Acknowledging progress encourages a continued commitment to time mastery.

Reflecting on any setbacks or challenges encountered provides valuable learning experiences. These reflections can guide future strategies and adjustments in time management practices.

Considering the skills and knowledge gained in the process, it highlights the broader benefits of time mastery. These benefits often extend beyond mere efficiency, contributing to personal growth and self-awareness.

Envisioning how this journey will continue to evolve sets the stage for ongoing improvement and adaptation. The time management journey is never truly complete; it's an ongoing process of learning and growth.

THE IMPACT OF EFFECTIVE TIME MANAGEMENT ON QUALITY OF LIFE

Mastering time management significantly improves life quality, bringing transformative changes across various life domains.

One of the foremost benefits is heightened productivity and efficiency, leading to both professional triumphs and personal gratification. Effectively managing time enables the completion of goals and tasks more proficiently, unlocking additional time for diverse activities.

Another key advantage is the reduction in stress and anxiety. Skillful time management alleviates the pressures associated with tight deadlines and overcommitment, fostering a more relaxed and enjoyable lifestyle.

Achieving a balanced work-life dynamic is a notable outcome of adept time management. Equitably juggling professional duties with personal interests and family time yields a more satisfying and well-rounded life experience.

Time management also sharpens focus and clarity, enhancing decision-making and problem-solving skills. This heightened mental acuity translates into more deliberate and impactful actions in both the personal and professional spheres.

Having greater control over one's schedule opens up space for self-care, leisure, and personal development. Mastery of time management empowers individuals to prioritize activities that nurture their well-being and encourage personal growth.

Overall, the sense of empowerment derived from effective time management is life-changing. It fosters a feeling of self-efficacy and competence, boosting self-esteem and cultivating a more optimistic perspective on life.

INTEGRATING TIME MANAGEMENT INTO EVERYDAY LIFE

To fully benefit from time management, it's crucial to integrate its principles into everyday life. This integration ensures that time management becomes a natural and seamless part of daily routines and decision-making.

Making time management a habitual practice involves incorporating its strategies into routine activities. Regular practice solidifies these habits, whether it's planning the day, prioritizing tasks, or setting goals.

Aligning time management practices with personal values and goals ensures that they are meaningful and motivating. This alignment ensures that time is spent on truly important and fulfilling activities.

Using time management tools and techniques consistently, from digital apps to traditional planners, aids in maintaining organization and focus. These tools become integral to managing daily tasks and commitments.

Adapting time management strategies to suit individual lifestyles and preferences ensures their effectiveness. The personalization of these strategies makes them more relevant and easier to maintain.

Teaching and sharing time management principles with family, friends, or colleagues can reinforce their application.

Teaching others not only benefits them but also strengthens one's own understanding and commitment to these practices.

Regularly reviewing and adjusting time management practices in response to changing circumstances or new insights ensures that they remain practical and relevant. This ongoing adjustment keeps time management strategies aligned with current needs and goals.

SETTING THE STAGE FOR CONTINUOUS IMPROVEMENT

Continuous improvement in time management is about consistently seeking ways to refine and enhance time management skills. This pursuit of excellence ensures that time management strategies evolve and adapt over time.

Setting specific goals for improvement in time management can provide direction and motivation. These goals can range from improving efficiency in specific tasks to achieving a better balance between work and personal life.

Seeking feedback from others on time management practices can offer new perspectives and ideas for improvement. This feedback can be invaluable, whether it's from colleagues, mentors, or family members.

Staying informed about new time management techniques and tools ensures that the latest and most effective strategies are used. Keeping up with developments in the field can lead to the discovery of new approaches that can enhance time management.

Experimenting with different time management methods and approaches can lead to more effective and personalized strategies. The willingness to try new techniques and adapt them to individual needs is vital to continuous improvement.

Reflecting regularly on the effectiveness of current time management practices helps identify areas for improvement. This reflection should be honest and objective, focusing on strengths and areas needing development.

Embracing a growth mindset, which views abilities and talents as developable rather than fixed, is crucial in pursuing continuous improvement. This mindset encourages a positive attitude towards learning and growth in time management.

EMPOWERING OTHERS THROUGH TIME MANAGEMENT

Imparting time management knowledge and skills to others can be incredibly impactful, whether in a professional context, within one's circle of family and friends, or across the broader community. Doing so can create a ripple effect, improving the overall ability to manage time efficiently within these groups.

Educating others on time management through structured training sessions, mentoring, or informal advice can yield significant benefits. This instruction not only aids individuals in enhancing their time management skills but also fosters a more efficient and productive collective environment.

Setting a positive example in time management can serve as inspiration and motivation for others. Showcasing effective time management techniques in real-life scenarios can be a compelling way to encourage others to adopt similar practices.

Developing resources or tools to aid others in time management, like guides, templates, or applications, offers practical support. These aids can be instrumental in helping others formulate and refine their own time management strategies.

Fostering a culture that emphasizes good time management, be it in a workplace or family setting, can lead to a more synchronized and efficient atmosphere. This environment nurtures shared values and practices focused on making the most of time.

Supporting and encouraging those who find time management challenging is crucial. Providing assistance, whether through sharing advice or resources or simply lending an ear, can make a substantial difference in their ability to manage their time effectively.

Reflecting on the effects of empowering others in time management underscores the value of these initiatives. Realizing the dual benefits of helping individuals and a wider group can be a strong incentive to continue promoting time management skills.

THE FUTURE OF TIME MANAGEMENT

Looking ahead to the future of time management involves anticipating how evolving technologies, societal changes, and personal aspirations will shape our approach to managing time. This forward-looking perspective can prepare us for future challenges and opportunities in time management.

Technological advancements, particularly in AI and automation, will likely significantly impact time management practices. These technologies can offer more efficient ways to manage tasks and schedules, but they require adaptability and a willingness to learn new skills.

The increasing emphasis on work-life integration rather than strict separation will influence future time management strategies. This shift reflects a more holistic view of work and life as interconnected components of a fulfilling existence.

Globalization and cultural diversity are reshaping our understanding of time management. Exposure to different cultural perspectives on time can offer valuable insights and alternative approaches to managing time effectively.

Environmental sustainability and social responsibility will become more integrated into time management practices. Managing time in ways that are not only efficient but also environmentally and socially responsible will become increasingly important.

Personalization and customization of time management tools and strategies will continue to evolve. Technology can offer more tailored solutions to individual time management challenges as it becomes more sophisticated.

Anticipating and preparing for these future trends and shifts ensures that our time management practices remain relevant and effective in an ever-changing world.

FINAL THOUGHTS: EMBRACING THE TIME WE HAVE

In wrapping up this exploration of time management, we recognize that its mastery extends beyond mere efficiency and productivity. It's about optimizing our time in a fulfilling and enriching manner. Embracing the time we have calls for a mindful and deliberate approach, aligning our use of time with our values, ambitions, and dreams.

Understanding time as a limited and valuable commodity encourages more thoughtful and meaningful use of it. Every moment matters, and making intentional choices about how we use our time can result in a meaningful and satisfying life.

Balancing immediate demands with future aspirations is a crucial element of truly embracing our time. While efficiency and productivity are essential, relishing the present and creating lasting memories are equally vital.

Regular reflection on our time usage and making necessary adjustments is pivotal to ensuring that our time management practices evolve with our changing needs and goals. This process of continual self-assessment and modification is essential for a rewarding use of time.

Sharing our time with others through kindness, quality moments with loved ones, or community involvement enriches its value. Time dedicated to others or in the company of those we care about is often the most gratifying.

Acknowledging that not every moment can or should be perfectly managed or productive is part of embracing our time. Allowing for spontaneity, rest, and unexpected delights is crucial for a balanced and joyful life.

Ultimately, time management is more than a collection of strategies or tools; it's a lifestyle choice. It's about making conscious decisions that resonate with our deepest values and aspirations, enabling us to live life fully and with meaning. This time management approach goes beyond being efficient; it embraces a fuller view of what it means to live a rich and rewarding life.

Embracing our time also means appreciating each moment and recognizing that our choices in spending our time define the quality of our lives. It's about finding joy in both the mundane and the extraordinary—in everyday tasks and once-in-a-lifetime experiences.

Thus, time management is an ongoing exploration, adaptation, and personal growth journey. It involves learning to navigate life's complexities with grace and intention. By mastering the art of time management, we enhance our lives and positively impact those around us.

As we move forward, we carry with us the lessons, strategies, and insights gained, applying them with insight and empathy. Let us embrace our time with gratitude, making every moment count towards a fulfilling life.

In short, mastering time is a continual practice that enriches our lives. By constantly refining our approach to time management, we open ourselves to new possibilities, greeting each day with enthusiasm and purpose. Let this journey in mastering time be transformative, guiding us towards a life filled with fulfillment and joy.

APPENDIX 1: THE POMODORO METHOD

The Pomodoro Technique is structured around intervals called "Pomodoros." Each Pomodoro consists of 25 minutes of focused work and a 5-minute break. These intervals are designed to provide a balanced rhythm of work and rest, maximizing concentration and minimizing burnout.

Implementation Steps

1. Choose a Task: Select a task or series of tasks you wish to work on.
2. Set the Timer: Use a timer to mark a 25-minute period dedicated exclusively to working on your chosen task.
3. Work on the Task: Focus solely on the task at hand until the timer rings. The idea is to work with full attention and without any interruptions.
4. Take a Short Break: After the timer goes off, take a 5-minute break. This brief respite allows your brain to

relax, making it easier to maintain focus over longer periods.

5. Repeat: After four Pomodoros, take a longer break of 15-30 minutes. These extended intervals help to recharge your mental energy.

Benefits

- Improved Focus and Concentration: By working in short bursts, the Pomodoro Technique helps maintain high levels of focus and concentration.
- Prevents Burnout: Regular breaks ensure that the mind doesn't get fatigued, reducing the risk of burnout.
- Enhanced Productivity: This method encourages a sense of urgency but within manageable timeframes, often leading to more work being done in less time.
- Minimizes Distractions: Committing to a task for a short period helps ward off distractions, as there's a clear end point in sight.
- Time Tracking: It provides a simple way to track the time spent on tasks, which can be insightful for future planning and time management.

Adaptability

One of the key strengths of the Pomodoro Technique is its adaptability. While the standard practice is 25-minute work intervals, individuals can adjust the lengths of both work and break periods to better fit their personal productivity rhythms. For tasks requiring deep concentration, longer Pomodoros might be more effective, while shorter intervals might suit more routine or fragmented tasks.

Summary

The Pomodoro Technique offers a structured yet flexible approach to managing time and workload. By breaking work into manageable intervals and interspersing them with short breaks, it helps maintain consistent productivity, manage cognitive load, and keep motivation high. Whether you're a student, professional, or anyone looking to enhance your time management skills, the Pomodoro Technique is a straightforward and practical tool to incorporate into your daily routine.

APPENDIX 2: THE EISENHOWER MATRIX

The Eisenhower Matrix

	URGENT	NOT URGENT
IMPORTANT	DO THIS	SCHEDULE THIS
NOT IMPORTANT	DELAGATE THIS	DELETE THIS

The Eisenhower Matrix, also known as the Urgent-Important Matrix, is a time management tool that helps prioritize tasks based on their urgency and importance. Dwight D. Eisenhower, who was well-known for his incredible capacity for sustained productivity, inspired the name of this matrix, which Stephen Covey popularized in his book "The 7 Habits of Highly Effective People."

Overview of the Eisenhower Matrix

The matrix is divided into four quadrants, each representing a different category of tasks based on two criteria: urgency and importance.

- Quadrant I: Urgent and Important (Do First)
- These tasks require immediate attention and are critical to your goals. They often have tight deadlines and significant consequences if not completed.
- Example: Crisis management, pressing deadlines, emergency situations.
- Quadrant II: Important but Not Urgent (Schedule)
- These tasks are important for long-term success and fulfillment but do not have an immediate deadline. They require planning and conscious effort to execute.
- Example: Personal development, long-term planning, relationship building.
- Quadrant III: Urgent but Not Important (Delegate)
- Tasks in this quadrant are usually interruptions from others and might not align with your personal goals. They seem urgent but are less important.
- Example: Most emails and phone calls, some meetings, minor requests from others.
- Quadrant IV: Neither Urgent nor Important (Delete)
- These are the least productive tasks, often serving as distractions. They neither contribute to your goals nor require immediate action.
- Example: Time-wasting activities, unnecessary meetings, trivial busy work.

How to Use the Eisenhower Matrix

1. List Down Tasks: Begin by listing all the tasks you need to do.
2. Categorize Each Task: Assign each task to one of the four quadrants based on its urgency and importance.
3. Prioritize and Action: Focus on tasks in Quadrant I first, as they are both urgent and important. Schedule time for Quadrant II tasks, as they are crucial for long-term success. Delegate Quadrant III tasks if possible, and try to minimize or eliminate tasks in Quadrant IV.

Benefits

- Enhanced Focus: By categorizing tasks, the matrix helps in distinguishing between what truly requires immediate attention and what can wait, leading to better focus and productivity.
- Improved Decision-Making: The matrix offers a clear framework for decision-making regarding the prioritization of tasks.
- Stress Reduction: By effectively managing urgent tasks and planning for important ones, it reduces stress and last-minute rushes.
- Balance: The matrix encourages a balance between urgent tasks and those that contribute to long-term goals, leading to more sustainable success and personal well-being.

Summary

The Eisenhower Matrix is a powerful tool for prioritizing tasks and managing time efficiently. By differentiating tasks based on urgency and importance, it helps individuals and teams focus on what truly matters, delegate appropriately, and avoid time-wasting activities. This strategy ensures that urgent daily needs do not take precedence over long-term objectives while also promoting productivity and a balanced approach to personal and professional life.

www.ingramcontent.com/pod-product-compliance
Lightning Source LLC
Chambersburg PA
CBHW070011300526
45794CB00001B/275